A SELF DEVELOPMENT PROGRAMME

Project Management

A SELF-DEVELOPMENT PROGRAMME

Project Management

THE ESSENTIAL GUIDE TO THINKING AND WORKING SMARTER

Peter Hobbs

MARSHALL PUBLISHING • LONDON

A Marshall Edition
Conceived, edited and
designed by
Marshall Editions Ltd
The Orangery
161 New Bond Street
London W1Y 9PA

First published in the UK
in 1999 by
Marshall Publishing Ltd

Copyright © 1999
Marshall Editions
Developments Ltd

ISBN 1-84028-280-0

Series Consultant Editor
Chris Roebuck
Managing Editor for
Axis Design
Jo Wells
Project Editor for
Axis Design
Theresa Reynolds
Design
Siân Keogh
at Axis Design
Art Director
Dave Goodman
Managing Art Editor
Patrick Carpenter
Managing Editor
Clare Currie
Editorial Assistant
Dan Green
Editorial Coordinator
Becca Clunes
Production
Amanda Mackie

Cover photography
Tony Stone Images

Originated in Italy by
Articolor
Printed and bound by
Printer Portuguesa

Contents

1

**Identifying projects
Setting priorities
Understanding roles
Self-assessment**

How can I make things go according to plan?
How much time can I spend on this?
Who has a stake in my project?

What is a project?

What do the Great Wall of China, the ceiling of the Sistine Chapel, the Apollo II moon landing, the Olympic Games, the 1985 "Live Aid" concert, Microsoft Windows and Viagra all have in common? They are all the results of successful projects.

Any piece of work is a project if it involves all of the following:
- a defined outcome
- resources (always people and nearly always other resources)
- a timescale

Projects can be about achieving a desired result, be it making a profit or building a bridge, or creating beneficial change – perhaps by developing new, more efficient working procedures.

Size is not important

Although high-profile projects may have workforces of hundreds, timescales measured in years and budgets running into billions, the same principles apply even if you are running a two-week project where you have the part-time support of one colleague and no formal budget at all.

The tools and techniques explained in this book will help you to achieve success in your projects. They apply to any size of project and are relevant whether or not project management is your main role, whether you are working mainly alone or managing a large team, and regardless of whether you have a computer and project scheduling software.

DO YOU NEED TO SHARPEN YOUR SKILLS?

Take a moment to consider whether any of the following statements apply to you. If so, then you can benefit from improving your project management skills.

- There are things I want to achieve in the next month/six months/year.
- My work involves grappling with large and complex tasks.
- I can see things around me that could be changed for the better.
- People look to me for leadership at work or at home.
- I find it difficult to convert ideas into action.
- I need people to work with me if I am to achieve what I want.
- I chair meetings where people spend time explaining why they haven't completed tasks and making unrealistic promises about the future!

Critical considerations

All projects involve the three factors of time, cost and quality. The relative importance of these will vary from one project to the next – if the purpose of a project is to generate profits, for example, then keeping costs low will be a high priority.

In some cases, one of the three will be fixed by circumstances and can therefore be said to be "critical" to success. In practice, of course, all three elements need to be kept under control for a project to be deemed successful.

Time critical

Event-planning projects are usually time-critical. In the case of a trade exhibition, for example, the deadline is immovable because the date of the event is fixed from the outset, a venue is booked and the place and date are widely advertised. Under these circumstances, moving the date back, even by a day, is simply not an option.

Quality critical

Some types of project demand that the outcome reach certain standards, even if this means that times extend and costs rise. In engineering and medical projects, for example, certain quality standards must be achieved before a product can be legally used.

Cost critical

Most commercial projects are cost-critical; that is, for the project to be a success it must stay within the budget set when the fee to be paid by the client was negotiated. If the fee is fixed and the project does not stay within its budget limits, it may lose money.

The time/cost/quality triangle

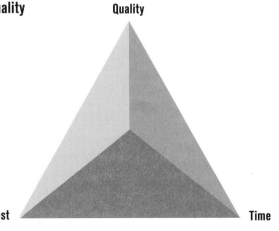

Quality

Cost

Time

Where do projects take place?

The study of project management usually takes place in a business context. However, projects are about creating beneficial change, so you will find them in every field of human endeavour.

Charities

Charities are reliant on profile and fundraising events to remain viable, and in many cases their humanitarian activities involve highly complex feats of planning and organization.

Sport

Bids for Olympic Games are now awarded seven years ahead of time to allow the hosting city to complete all the preparations. These cost billions of dollars and involve the coordinated effort of thousands of people.

Politics

National election campaigns in most democracies last between three and six months, but the planning and fundraising required for success will have begun years ahead.

Engineering

Every branch of engineering uses projects as the means by which vision is turned into reality. The project sequence is equally relevant whether you are building a road, a printed circuit board, a ship or an aeroplane.

Research and development

Today universities receive a large proportion of their funding against tightly defined research briefs. In addition, large organizations often maintain their own research and development departments to work on the projects that will give them future competitive advantage.

At home

We all carry out projects in our daily lives. Carrying out major home improvements, organizing a holiday or planning a surprise party for a family member, for example, are projects involving time, resources and outcomes, although we might not think of them in these terms.

PROJECT-BASED ORGANIZATIONS
In an increasingly competitive global economy, the companies that thrive are those who have both the vision to identify their clients' needs and the flexibility to meet them most fully, quickly and cost-effectively. In service industries, particularly those such as advertising or design where there is a high degree of creativity required, companies have replaced old-fashioned management hierarchies with newer, more flexible structures that allow them to pull together project teams from across functions to focus on the needs of the customer.

Projects and priorities

Many people are given project management responsibilities at work alongside their everyday tasks. One of the challenges in these circumstances is to maintain a focus on what is important in the face of the urgent demands that inevitably crop up every day.

Reactive and proactive working

Everyone's job combines reactive and proactive working. On a day-to-day basis, things will crop up that need our immediate attention – such as phone calls or urgent client requests. In addition, most people have longer-term development tasks to complete. These are not urgent today, but at some point will become so if you leave them undone. Maximum productivity at work is gained by planning ahead in a proactive way.

Striking a balance

The diagram below sets out the relationship between importance and urgency and identifies categories of activity. Getting a correct balance between the four quadrants is central to good time management. Projects contain elements of all four quadrants, but in their entirety should be seen as high importance, low urgency (H2) tasks. They may have to take second place to high importance, high urgency (H1) crises, but every effort should be made to prevent L1 distractions (such as unimportant phone calls) from shunting them into third place.

When setting priorities at work, remember to consider importance and urgency separately. They are NOT the same thing.

	REACTIVE	PROACTIVE
high	**H1** Crises or fleeting opportunities	**H2** Development tasks (projects)
low	**L1** Distractions	**L2** Maintenance tasks
	high (1)	low (2)

IMPORTANCE

URGENCY

Project and priorities

SELF-ASSESSMENT EXERCISE

1 Record your activities in the course of a typical working day day using a simple time log (activity, duration)

2 Draw a simple four-quadrant matrix like the one on the previous page, and allocate each activity to one of the quadrants in the matrix according to its urgency and importance.

3 Calculate what percentage of your time was spent in each quadrant.

4 Add the percentages of time spent in the high-urgency quadrants H1 and L1 to give you your "reactivity quotient".

INTERPRETING THE RESULT
Different jobs will naturally incorporate more reactivity than others (a "help desk" operator will always be more reactive than a research scientist). The value of identifying your reactivity quotient is that it gives you a logical basis for calculating the additional time you will need to complete proactive tasks. For example, if your job is 75 percent reactive, a task requiring two hours' effort will take eight hours to complete.

Becoming more proactive

If you take on a project at work, you will need a proactive approach to ensure that it is not constantly at the bottom of your list of priorities. The following tips can help you to do this.

■ Agree to take on a project only if you are prepared to make sacrifices to get it done.

■ Take time in the planning phase to identify what needs to be done and how long it will take.

■ When planning your project timetable, be sure to make a realistic assessment of how reactive you generally have to be at work, using the self-assessment exercise. Add in time for that reactivity.

■ Book in regular blocks of time for project work. Allocate specific activities to these.

■ Enlist the aid of your managers and colleagues. Tell them what you are planning to do and discuss the implications for your job and theirs.

■ Find someone to act as your "project coach", helping you to set targets, solve problems and review progress.

The project life cycle

Project management in its simplest form is a sequence of activities that follow a logical order. The sequence is the same whatever the circumstances.

Definition

The first step is to identify what you want to achieve, by when and within what cost constraints. This process is sometimes called "scoping" or "specing". This is the point at which you decide the relative importance of time, cost and quality.

Planning

Most projects consist of a number of tasks. By planning you can ensure that you have a clear idea of what these are and the order in which they can best be done. Planning is also an opportunity to confirm that the project as defined is likely to be achievable . The planning stage may involve some repetition of the definition stage – the plan making it clearer what is possible within time and cost constraints.

Implementation

Once the plan is in place, you are in a position to begin working towards your goal. The implementation process also includes opportunities to monitor progress and adjust the plan as necessary. Communication and people management become very important at this stage.

Handover

The result of the project needs to be handed over to those who will be using it. This will normally require them to modify their behaviour in some way, which in turn may mean having to learn new skills. The handover phase concentrates on all these issues.

Review

Projects are an excellent opportunity for corporate and individual learning. You can maximize the benefits of this by looking back on what you have done to get a balanced view of what you have learned, and implement actions to incorporate this into future projects.

Roles in and around projects

When you are asked to lead a project, one of your main tasks will probably be to coordinate the efforts of a team. You will need to define who is fulfilling what role in your project, and who has a stake in the process and final outcome. A stakeholder is anyone who can affect, or is affected by, the process or outcome of the project. Stakes can be positive, neutral or negative. In a project to reorganize a company, those likely to be promoted will generally be positive, and those whose status is diminished will tend to be negative.

The diagram shows roles you might have in your project. In some cases people will play more than one role. The key relationships on the diagram are between the project sponsor, client/end user and project manager. Poor communication between any of these three increases the risk of a project delivering an unsatisfactory result.

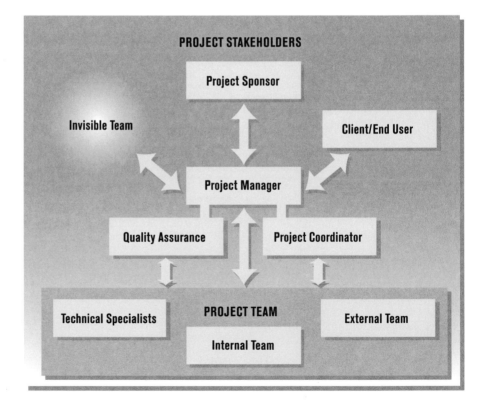

The project sponsor

The project sponsor is the person on whose authority a project takes place. This means that they are the ultimate arbiter of whether the project has succeeded or failed. The sponsor also has authority over the resources required for successful completion. The sponsor should "champion" the project within the stakeholder group and acts as mentor or coach to the project manager and team.

The sponsor's tasks

The sponsor is involved at all stages of the project, and in particular should:

- agree the specification, signing off any project definition document
- review any initial plans
- agree the escalation procedure – that is, the circumstances in which they should be informed or involved when things go wrong
- conduct regular reviews of progress through the implementation phase
- authorize all changes to the project scope during implementation
- conduct or oversee quality assurance reviews
- authorize handover of the completed product
- conduct or oversee final project review

The sponsor is the only person who can terminate a project.

Choosing a sponsor

On occasions where the project manager is in a position to choose a project sponsor, availability and authority are two important factors to take into account.

- The ideal sponsor should be contactable at a moment's notice and have the time to take an active interest in progress.
- The more powerful the sponsor, the less likely it is that your project will run into opposition.

There usually has to be some trade-off between these two factors. Sponsors at senior level will often be too busy to be intimately aware of the progress of a project. More junior sponsors tend to have more time, but often lack the authority to be taken seriously by the wider stakeholder goup.

The project manager

The project manager is responsible for the day-to-day running of the project. They are at the centre of the communications diagram and the success of the project will to a large extent rely on their ability and enthusiasm. Ideally the project manager will be involved in "scoping", and will have the opportunity to meet the clients and end users. Skilful project managers will identify key stakeholders at the outset of the project and take active steps to harness positive stakes and minimize the effect of negative ones.

The project manager's tasks

The project manager is responsible for:

- preparing project plans
- building a strong team
- motivating individuals
- defining roles and setting objectives for team members
- scheduling control points and milestones
- monitoring progress of work against plans
- keeping the sponsor appropriately informed at all times
- preparing reports on progress as required
- ensuring smooth passage of information throughout the project hierarchy
- representing the needs of the project to the stakeholder group
- documenting all changes to the original specification
- conducting regular learning reviews

EIGHT PARADOXES OF PROJECT MANAGEMENT

According to the American management guru Tom Peters, there are eight key paradoxes in a good project manager. The truly successful project manager needs to be able to balance the qualities in the left-hand column with their opposites on the right:

1

TOTAL EGO
Confident in his/her own ability and right to make demands of people.

NO EGO
Not one to pull rank – a true servant leader.

2

AUTOCRAT
Decisive and authoritative where necessary.

DELEGATOR
Encourages team members to act on their own initiative.

3

LEADER
Has a vision of the future and inspires people.

MANAGER
Manages the nuts and bolts of implementation.

4

COMFORTABLE WITH AMBIGUITY
Projects are surrounded by ambiguity. Searching for exactitudes causes paralysis.

OBSESSED WITH PRECISION
Some things do need precise definition. The project manager has a nose for what these are.

5

GOOD FACE-TO-FACE COMMUNICATOR
Is confident and persuasive in face-to-face briefings. Builds rapport with people.

GOOD COMMUNICATOR IN WRITING
Has the discipline to write things down and ensures paperwork is kept up to date.

6

UNFAZED BY COMPLEXITY
Recognizes that the direct route is not always the best one.

LIKES TO KEEP THINGS SIMPLE
Believes that simple rules are most likely to be kept and simple solutions most often work.

7

AWARE OF THE BIG PICTURE
Is able to take account of the environment (political, economic or business) that surrounds the project.

ATTENTION TO DETAIL
Pays attention to the small but vital components of a project that can mean the difference between failure and success.

8

IMPATIENT
A project manager often needs to agitate to overcome resistance and achieve a result.

PATIENT
Sometimes listening is more effective than speaking. Unnecessary checking slows progress.

Clients and end users

Since it is the client who will be taking delivery of the final product of the project, this person or group should be extensively consulted in the definition phase. Although the sponsor signs off the definition, the needs of the end user should decide what goes into it.

The elusive end user

The client and the end user are often not the same. For example, in the case of building a new road, the client would be the local authority, not the motorists who will use the road. Generally speaking, if you please the end user the client also ends up satisfied.

In some projects it is surprisingly difficult to speak to the end user. This may be due to the sensitive nature of what is proposed, but more often is due to over-zealous "gate-keepers" within organizations who claim to speak on behalf of the end user group. It may depend on the quality of consultation and the willingness of the end user to get involved. For example, in the case of a proposed new road, it may be easier to get input from people who object to it than from those who might wish to use it. The project manager will find ways around these problems.

Consulting the end user

It may be necessary to carry out some market research as a preliminary to your project. You may also decide to produce a prototype to show what is planned. From that point until final handover the project manager should keep clients and end users informed of progress. In the latter stages of the project this may mean training them in any new skills required.

In some projects there are a variety of end users with different stakes in the outcome. For example, a new computer system may be used to monitor a process within a factory. Some end users will input data, others might have to work with it and a third group might have to make decisons based on the information produced by it.

The project manager should recognize each distinct group and tailor communication accordingly. In the example just described, the first group could be hostile to having their performance monitored and have a negative view; the second group might have to take on additional responsibilities but be relatively neutral. But the management group who work with the output will probably be very positive.

The project team

The make-up of the project team will vary considerably according to the nature and context of the project. Typically, however, it will fall into three sub-groups:

- technical specialists
- external team
- internal team

Each group needs to be managed in a different way.

Technical specialists

Team members with specialist technical knowledge are usually employed as consultants. They tend to be expensive and can often offer only limited time to your project. They should therefore be given a very specific brief or used to oversee or advise on more general matters.

External team

You may be able to outsource certain parts of project to other organizations. You will probably need to come to a formal agreement about the timescales, scope and cost of work. Provided you get the initial agreement right, you will rarely need to become involved in the day-to-day management of outsourced contracts. If you get it wrong, on the other hand, correcting it later can be time-consuming and expensive.

Internal team

Members of your internal team tend to come from your own organization or department, so you will generally find yourself adopting a less formal style when delegating tasks to them. Beware, however, of equating a less formal style with a less tight definition of what is required or by when. This is particularly crucial when delegating to more senior members of the team.

Often the internal team is the most difficult group to manage because its members are busy with other things and do your project work as a "favour". The advantages of the internal team are that there is rarely an out-of-pocket cost associated with using it, and its members' strengths and weaknesses are generally known to the project manager.

When thinking about project team members and whether tasks should be outsourced or done internally, there are some key questions that you need to ask yourself.

- Do we need constant access to this person's skills?
- Will they be needed at every stage of the project?
- Does our organization have the expertise to carry out this function?
- Are potential internal candidates already heavily committed elsewhere?

Other project roles

Quality assurance

Many companies have quality assurance standards in place that require projects to follow set procedures. The quality assurance team will audit the process of the project at agreed points in its life cycle. If there is no designated team responsible for this, the project manager should take on this role.

Project coordinator

In larger projects there may be a designated coordinator responsible for administration on behalf of the project manager. In smaller projects, the coordination role is another one that falls to the project manager.

Invisible team

The term "invisible team" was coined by the author Geoff Reiss in his book *Project Management De-mystified*. He uses it to describe all the factors that may have an effect (generally, but not always, a negative one) on the progress of your project. I have included it as part of the diagram on page 14 because in some projects it is useful to view these factors as stakeholders that can have an impact on your plans.

For example, a road construction project might have to factor in the weather and school holidays when creating a schedule of work. Both would be good examples of "invisible team" members.

Checklist for current projects

You may already be involved in a number of projects at work. If so, you may find it helpful to start thinking about these in a more structured way, particularly with regard to your own role and the roles of any other people involved. If you are involved in several projects, make copies of the checklist and use a separate one for each project.

PROJECT ASSESSMENT CHECKLIST

1 What project am I currently involved in?

_____

_____

2 What are the time/cost/quality parameters of this project?

Time _____

Cost _____

Quality _____

3 What proportion of my time at work is reactive? (See page 12 for guidelines on how to work this out).

_____ percent

4 Of my remaining (proactive time), what proportion can I allocate to this project ?

_____ percent

5 What role am I playing in this project? (You may have more than one role – for example, project manager and quality assurance).

_____

6 Who are the other people in my project team?

_____

_____

7 Who is in the following roles?:

Sponsor _____

Manager _____

Client/End user _____

8 Who are the major stakeholders in my project? Are their stakes positive, neutral or negative?

Stakeholder	Pos/Neg/Neutral
_____	_____
_____	_____

2

Analyse costs and benefits

Define objectives

Initiate action

Identify stakeholders' views

How can I make this idea happen?
Who needs to be involved?
What will the benefits be?

Project initiation

How a project is initiated will depend largely on the type of organization carrying out the project and the level of authority of the person who originated the idea.

Commercial projects

These days, much of the trade between commercial organizations takes the form of projects. Sales forces sell the benefits of some change or other, attaching a price tag and a time frame that they believe can be met profitably through good project management.

Ironically, many of these companies separate sales or account management from operations or project management. This can mean that the project is effectively being initiated by the sales team, who may agree to unrealistically high specifications, low budgets or short time frames which cannot be met by the project management teams. This results in customer dissatisfaction, unprofitable trading and recrimination between departments.

This is often no more than a simple communication problem that can be overcome by involving project managers earlier in the sales process. (Of course, this can only be done if they have the interpersonal and commercial skills to cope!)

Change projects

Projects that are initiated within an organization for its own purposes are often change projects; they may be intended to develop new working practices or find new sources of business. Generally speaking, change projects are initiated in one of two ways: "top down" or "bottom up".

"Top down"

A project is initiated "top down" when an organization or sponsor at a senior level identifies a need and appoints a project manager to work on it. Progressive organizations often have dedicated structures to generate, evaluate and allocate new project ideas.

"Bottom up"

A project is initiated "bottom up" when the idea comes from someone who is not sufficiently senior to take the decision to implement it. Anyone can have a good project idea, and there is no reason why the idea should not become a reality if the originator can get support for it.

STRENGTHS	WEAKNESSES
"TOP DOWN" PROJECTS	■ Many pointless projects are generated in this way. Because they began life as the brainchild of a senior executive, no-one has questioned their value until time and resources have been committed.
■ Ideas that are generated "top down" often have funds allocated to them from the start.	■ The project manager may only become involved after initial scoping, which can reduce their level of ownership. This leads either to the project failing or the sponsor getting more involved than they should be.
■ Having a clearly defined structure for initiating projects means that there is a clear procedure for people to follow when they want to present new project ideas.	
"BOTTOM UP" PROJECTS	
■ Ideas born at junior levels within an organization are generally better validated before they become projects.	■ Unless the initiator knows how to generate support for their project, it may fail no matter what its merit.
■ If the originator of the idea is also the project manager, they will be more motivated to see it succeed	

Making "bottom up" initiation work

- **What is unique about your idea?**
- **What benefits can it offer to your organization?**
- **Who can help you to refine it?**
- **To whom can you sell it?**
- **Can they help you sell it to others?**

Too many good ideas fail because they remain the brainchild of one individual. Here are several things you can do to assess the quality of your initial ideas and make that vital step between a good idea and a workable one.

1 Involve others

Many projects fail to become reality because the people with the original ideas keep them to themselves. They may do this for any of a number of reasons – typical reasons are fear of losing control and fear of having their ideas "shot down". However, all but the most limited projects will affect other people, and unless you take steps to win their understanding and support, the project is almost bound to fail. Some ideas for involving people in the preliminary stages of the project are given on page 27.

2 Find a sponsor

Unless you have the authority to sponsor the project yourself, you will need to identify and approach someone to fill this role. To do this, you may have to spend time putting together a selling document or presentation. The central strand of your proposal should usually be a cost/benefit analysis.

3 Allow others to build on your idea

On occasion the originator of an idea prevents its realization by refusing to allow others to modify it in any way. Not only can other people help to test the idea and improve its quality, but they will also feel more motivated to work on your project if they feel at least part-ownership of it.

4 Don't give up

According to Einstein, "If an idea does not have some element of absurdity at the outset, it probably isn't worth pursuing." Unfortunately, seemingly mad ideas are more difficult to sell to the people you need to make them reality, so you will need to persevere. Many revolutionary ideas, such as Post-it notes or the clockwork radio, have only come into being because of the persistence of their inventors. If you think you have a good idea, don't allow initial rejection to stand in your way.

How to involve others

The earlier you involve others in your idea, the more support you are likely to generate. Giving people the opportunity to make a contribution to your project in the initial stages will increase their level of commitment throughout. There are several ways you can do this.

Run a brainstorming session

The purpose of a brainstorming session is to generate as many solutions as possible. First, state the problem. Next, encourage everyone present to come up with solutions, however unorthodox.

Only once you have generated a large number of solutions should you begin evaluating the merits of each. The chosen solution is often an amalgam of many people's ideas.

Conduct a forcefield analysis

This method of analysing a problem was first developed by the management theorist Professor Kurt Lewin in 1951. He suggests that the status quo is the point of equilibrium between driving and restraining forces operating in any given situation. A forcefield analysis identifies the restraining forces so a plan can then be created to either weaken or remove them. It provides a model that lends itself to group discussion. Project managers may use it as a way to identify problems, which can then be resolved using the brainstorming approach described above.

Conduct research among end users

At its most complex level, this may involve commissioning sophisticated market research. On a smaller scale, it could mean a conversation with one or a number of end-users to determine their needs in a particular area or their attitudes to what you propose.

Carry out a cost/benefit analysis

This is an objective analysis of the likely costs and benefits of a project, leading to a decision on whether or not to go ahead. (See pages 28–29.)

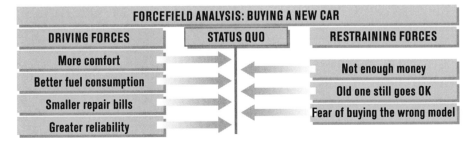

FORCEFIELD ANALYSIS: BUYING A NEW CAR

DRIVING FORCES	STATUS QUO	RESTRAINING FORCES
More comfort		Not enough money
Better fuel consumption		Old one still goes OK
Smaller repair bills		Fear of buying the wrong model
Greater reliability		

Cost/benefit analysis

A cost/benefit analysis is a means of weighing up whether the project is worth embarking upon. Originally it was a purely financial tool, and both cost and benefit were described in monetary terms. In many projects, however, the desired benefits are less easily measurable matters such as quality of life or levels of morale. Regardless of the nature of the benefits, an analysis should be carried out to help you decide whether it is worth going ahead with your project.

Costs

Ultimately the costs of a project should be assessed in financial terms. It is important to take account of both "out-of-pocket" (OOP) costs, such as the cost of materials or sub-contracted services, and invisible costs, such as the cost of your time and that of other internal team members.

When costing a project you will normally note only those costs that relate to it and not the general overheads that would be incurred by the business regardless of whether the project were being undertaken or not.

Benefits

You will usually have a good idea what the benefits of your project will be. The challenge is to quantify the nature and scale of the benefit.

To get a true picture, you need also to consider the point at which the benefits can be expected. In some cases a small return in the short term is preferable to a larger one that will take longer to come to fruition.

Another important issue to take into account is risk. Projected benefits can rarely be guaranteed and so your analysis should contain an assessment of what could go wrong and the effect of this on the overall outcome. (For more information on assessing risk, see pages 47–49).

MAKING THE DECISION

Once you have created a framework for understanding both costs and benefits in financial terms you should be in a position to decide whether the project is worth embarking upon. There is no standard method for doing this; many organizations apply accounting formulas such as Return on Capital Employed (ROCE), payback periods or Discounted Cash Flows (DCFs) to any investment decisions. Even if you have an accountancy background and feel confident you can use these formulas on your own, always try to get your organization's finance department involved. By doing this, you can often turn your sternest critic into a champion for the expenditure you propose. Ultimately the decision needs to be taken by the sponsor.

Asking "Why?"

While costs are relatively easy to measure, quantifying the potential benefits of a project is usually more difficult. One way of testing whether your goal is in line with the broader aims of your organization is to subject it to a technique known as "the five Whys?".

The question "Why?" can be answered in one of two ways:

- "Because..."
- "In order to..." (with variations "To..." and "So that...")

"Because" usually introduces a reactive reason for doing something. "In order to" looks to the future and usually introduces a proactive answer.

The challenge with "the five Whys?" is to follow a proactive chain of logic through five successive stages. As a rule, if the sequence does not lead to one of your organization's strategic goals within the five steps then the project is probably not worth pursuing.

Further testing

To gain maximum benefit from this process you should now ask the following supplementary questions:

- Is the logic in this sequence flawed at any stage?
- To what extent will the project under consideration contribute to the strategic goal?

- Are there any other projects that will also contribute?
- What might be the "unintended consequences"? In the example below, if it becomes easier to arrange meetings, is it possible that matters that should be dealt with by individuals will be deferred to a meeting, resulting in a *slower* decision-making process?

By making your reasoning explicit in this way you can often identify benefits that can be quantified, perhaps in terms of cash, resources, salary or new business opportunities.

The most revealing question you can ask is "Why?" Never undertake a project for which you cannot identify an "in order to" answer to the question "Why?" Ideally your project should stand up to the five "Whys?" test.

FIVE REASONS WHY

The following is an example of the five "Why's?" used to test a project to develop a computerized diary system:

Q. Why do we need a computerized diary system?
A. In order to coordinate meetings within the group.

Q. Why do we need to coordinate meetings within the group?
A. In order to make decisions more quickly.

Q. Why do we need to be able to make decisions more quickly?
A. In order to respond more quickly to our clients' needs.

Q. Why do we need to respond to our clients' needs more quickly?
A. In order to beat our competitors to contracts.

Q. Why do we need to beat our competitors to contracts?
A. In order to increase our revenue in line with growth targets.

Defining the project

A clear project definition must refer not only to the objective but also to a definite timescale and a fixed amount of money or resources: the three points of the quality–cost–time triangle (see page 9).

The definition process involves fixing each of these three parameters in a way that will allow you and all other stakeholders to refer back to them in the future.

How flexible should the definition be?

One of the excuses often given for fudging the definition process is that in a changing environment we do not know exactly what we will need by the time the project is complete, so things are deliberately kept vague to allow flexibility in the future.

This is a dangerous misconception. Fixing parameters does not mean that they have to remain set in stone until completion, but clarity in the definition is an essential platform upon which to base future changes. Flexibility should involve a willingness to make changes later if necessary, not an unwillingness to set parameters in the first place.

Who should set the definition?

The production of a clear and agreed definition of what constitutes success should be the first priority of the project manager.

Ideally the whole project team and all the key stakeholders should be involved. This will tend to maximize ownership and reduce the likelihood of misunderstandings. Often, however, there are practical reasons why this is not possible.

Key questions

The key questions address the issues of time, cost and quality. The first two questions are fairly straightforward.
■ Time: how long have we got?
■ Cost: how much can we spend?
However, addressing the issue of quality in the definition is far more tricky.

SETTING THE CHALLENGE

A clearly defined objective should have the same effect on a project team as the peak of a distant mountain has to a group of climbers: some will instantly know they want to take up the challenge and feel nothing but excitement. Others may feel daunted by the enormity of what lies ahead. A third group may know instinctively that it is not for them. A clear goal demands a clear choice: by setting it out clearly at the outset you can remove any weak links before they fail under pressure.

Quality

Defining quality in a project is a combination of art and science. Success depends on asking the right people the right questions, understanding the responses and recording them in an easily accessible format. In some projects, particularly in internal change projects, you may find it helpful to conduct a detailed stakeholder analysis: that is, identify everyone who could be affected by your project and establish their attitude. You may be able to speak to all stakeholders individually, but in large projects getting the views of a representative sample may be more practical.

ASKING THE RIGHT PEOPLE: STAKEHOLDER ANALYSIS

Brainstorm to identify all the people affected by your project. Identify their level of influence, assigning them to one of two categories:

■ **HIGH INFLUENCE**
Support critical to success; opposition will prevent success

■ **LOW INFLUENCE**
Support desirable but not essential, or will not influence success

Meet with all major stakeholder groups to assess their attitude towards your project, assigning them to one of three categories:

■ **POSITIVE**
Committed to or positive about the process and outcome

■ **NEUTRAL**
No strong feelings either way

■ **NEGATIVE**
Generally negative about or opposed to the process and outcome

Make plans to maintain positive stakes, move neutral stakeholders to positive and neutralize any negatives, making a priority of high-influence stakeholders. You may find it helpful to draw a matrix like the one shown here, assigning each stakeholder group to one of the boxes.

	HIGH INFLUENCE, POSITIVE ATTITUDE	LOW INFLUENCE, POSITIVE ATTITUDE
POSITIVE	Maintain this person's support. Example: MD very keen, involve as much as possible and keep informed.	Maintain this person's support. Example: Secretary very positive and willing to help. Involve and try to find a role on team.
NEUTRAL	HIGH INFLUENCE, NEUTRAL ATTITUDE Try to make them positive. Example: Senior management team non-committal. Arrange a brief presentation to explain the benefits and invite their input.	LOW INFLUENCE, NEUTRAL ATTITUDE Move to positive if possible, but don't spend too much time or effort. Example: Freelance staff not interested – discuss with them informally and invite suggestions.
NEGATIVE	HIGH INFLUENCE, NEGATIVE ATTITUDE Try to move to neutral or positive. Example: Finance director sceptical. Involve them in creating the cost/benefit analysis.	LOW INFLUENCE, NEGATIVE ATTITUDE Try to move to neutral or positive. Example: Packers worried about job losses as result of project. Do brief presentation to reassure them.

Quality

Opposition to projects is often based on misconceptions or bruised egos. By all means take into account the views of those who oppose your project, but unless they are end users, be wary of adjusting the scope of the project to satisfy their needs.

Asking the right questions

To get the most from questioning your stakeholders, avoid asking questions that can be answered with a simple "Yes" or "No". Questions beginning "What?", "Why?", "Who?", "How?", "Where?" and "When?" will elicit more detailed and informative answers. The following are examples of some of the questions you might ask.

What?

■ What exactly is the result required?
■ What resources do we need?

Why?

■ Why is this result required?
■ Why is it required now?

Who?

■ Who are the end users of the result?
■ Who will support it?
■ Who will manage it?

How?

■ How will it be implemented?
■ How long will it be in use?

Where?

■ Where will it be used?

When?

■ When will it be used?
■ When will it cease to be useful?

Recording project definition

Once you are clear on what you have to achieve, make sure that you record your definition in a format that makes it accessible for review throughout the life span of the project.

Although the specification in a large and complex project may need to run into hundreds of pages, experienced project managers often find it useful to produce a summary in one or two pages to act as their prime point of reference. An example of a project definition summary is given opposite. You may want to use this format, or simply incorporate some of its features into your own project definition form. If you feel uncomfortable with so formal a document, you may find it useful to minute what has been agreed in the form of a letter or memo that can be circulated to key stakeholders.

PROTOTYPING

In many instances the client/end user groups you are talking to will have a less than fully formed idea of what they want. In this case the definition process should be a dialogue. Their initial ideas can be used to create a prototype which is then presented back to them for further feedback.

PROJECT NAME	PROJECT IDENTIFICATION CODE
Project Lazarus	15a–d/99

SUB-PROJECTS Felix, Telstar, K2, Rubicon

PROJECT MANAGER:	PROJECT SPONSOR
J. Fisher, Call Centre Manager	M. Warp, Vice-President

END USER(S)
Call centre staff in Brighton and Milton Keynes

BENEFITS 15 percent increased revenue per operator

SCOPE/OBJECTIVES

Essentials:	Desirables:
– Reduce query response times	– Automated management reports
– Remove need to call customers back	– No more than 2 hours' training required

TIMINGS Roll out complete: Brighton, June; Milton Keynes, September

COST/RESOURCES
Total budget £300k. Programming £200k; staff training £80k; project support £20k.

PARAMETERS	ASSUMPTIONS
No interruptions in call centre operations	Network upgrade complete by end March

AUTHORITY LEVELS
Sponsor to sign all expenditure over £10k
Sponsor to be informed of any variance greater than 10 percent

AGREEMENT

SPONSOR	PROJECT MANAGER

3

Identify tasks
Estimate timescales
Allocate responsibilities
Assess risks

What is the project supposed to deliver?
What is the logical sequence of tasks?
Who will do what and when?

Planning: an overview

Planning is a means of creating a mental model of what lies ahead of us. It allows us to anticipate the need for resources and maximize our chances of success. The plan is a route map by which the project manager navigates and measures progress. It should be consulted and updated regularly, at the very least during every review meeting. The project manager should take every opportunity to familiarize the team with its detail.

The planning sequence

The following is the usual sequence by which a project plan is created.

- State the scope and objectives of the project. The detail of this will have been worked out during the definition stage.

PLAN TO SAVE MONEY

As a project progresses, costs rise and room for manoeuvre rapidly decreases. Although the project manager should always be prepared to amend the plan if appropriate, a well-thought out plan should prevent a situation where major changes become necessary when a great deal of money has already been invested and options are severely limited.

- Identify the deliverables that will achieve this. For example, a company building houses to sell might identify the following deliverables: planning permission, finances, building, utilities, marketing.
- Identify the tasks that must be carried out to produce the deliverables. For example, to obtain planning permission, the tasks might be: fill out planning application, attend meeting with planning authority, negotiate any changes required.
- Identify the timescales and resources required to do these tasks.
- Identify the dependencies between tasks. (See page 41 for more about dependencies.)
- Allocate responsibilities for tasks.
- Refine the plan by assessing risk, setting review milestones and so on.

Having identified exactly what you want to achieve, next create a detailed plan of how you will get this result. Include a breakdown of all the tasks, timescales and responsibilities.

Failure to plan

A common mistake people make is not planning in the interests of flexibility. This is based on the misperception that a plan, once formulated, must be followed slavishly through to its completion. Another reason people feel unable to plan is that they do not know enough about the future. No matter what project you are involved in, your plan will always be an approximation based on less than complete information. But if you know what you want to achieve, as you should if you have carried out the definition process, you have enough information to make a plan worthwhile.

BEWARE "EXECUTIVE WALLPAPER"
In some projects, a diligently crafted plan, using all the finest features of the most up-to-date project management software sits behind the project manager's desk as a status symbol. Once completed, this plan is largely ignored throughout the rest of the project and has little or no relevance to work in progress. It is no more than rather pretentious wall decoration.

Creating a plan

VIDEO ARTS

"Plan the process"

The first step in creating a detailed plan is to develop a Deliverable Breakdown Structure (DBS) and Work Breakdown Structure (WBS). The DBS is simply a breakdown of all the deliverables – things that the project needs to produce – some of which may have been identified in the initial definition phase; the WBS is a breakdown of all the tasks required to produce the deliverables.

Producing the DBS and WBS

Although the DBS and WBS are different, you may find you start to generate the two simultaneously.

Both start with a creative phase, and continue with a logical phase in which you evaluate and order the ideas produced. The basic materials for the process outlined below are:

■ Post-it notes
■ pens
■ whiteboard (or use a flip chart or any convenient flat surface)

Order of work

1 Re-state briefly what it is you want to achieve as a result of your definition phase. This should include any constraints you are aware of.

2 Take a Post-it pad and write on each sheet anything you might need to produce (for DBS) or might need to do (for WBS). Do not attempt any evaluation at this point; just generate ideas as quickly as possible. Speed often has the effect of increasing creativity.

For a DBS, the Post-its should refer to tangible objects – nouns. For a WBS, Post-its should contain activities – verbs. In practice, you may find yourself confusing the two, but don't let this restrict the flow of ideas.

3 Stick completed Post-its on the whiteboard/flip chart. Do not worry about duplication. Try to produce as many Post-its as possible.

4 Once you have run out of ideas, divide the deliverables from the tasks. At this stage you may find that you need to write additional Post-its.

5 Look for patterns by which you can group your Post-its. With the DBS, the usual logic is to identify a hierarchy of deliverables, creating sub-groups under the main deliverables. In the WBS, the patterns may relate to the order in which tasks should be carried out, or groups of tasks that will be done by the same individual or department. Again, this process may generate some new Post-its.

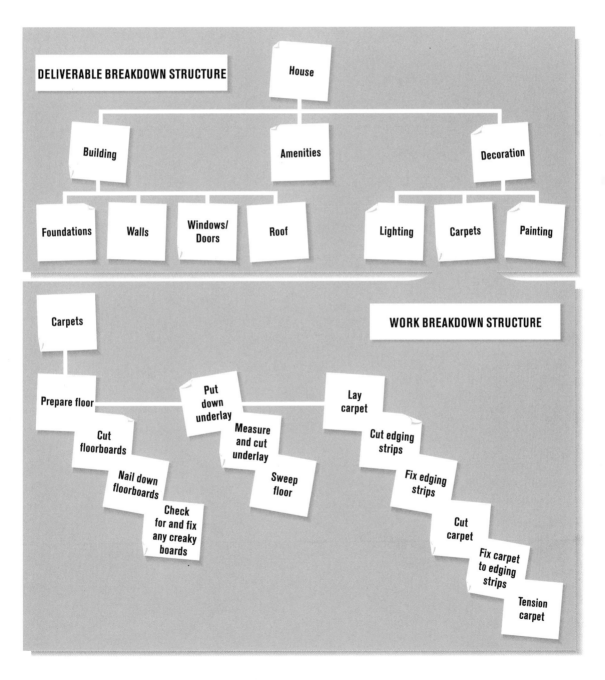

DELIVERABLE BREAKDOWN STRUCTURE

House

Building

Amenities

Decoration

Foundations

Walls

Windows/ Doors

Roof

Lighting

Carpets

Painting

WORK BREAKDOWN STRUCTURE

Carpets

Prepare floor

Put down underlay

Lay carpet

Cut floorboards

Measure and cut underlay

Cut edging strips

Nail down floorboards

Sweep floor

Fix edging strips

Check for and fix any creaky boards

Cut carpet

Fix carpet to edging strips

Tension carpet

From WBS to activity plan

Having identified in detail as many of the work elements as you can at this stage, you can begin to create a plan for completing the work in the most efficient way by carrying out the following steps:

- identify any irrelevant tasks
- identify the resources needed for each task
- decide how long each task will take
- identify its relationship to other tasks in the plan

1 Identify any irrelevant tasks

On occasion you may have to discount elements or whole branches of your DBS and WBS as falling outside the scope of your present project. You may also need to rewrite Post-its to clarify exactly what needs to be done, divide tasks into sub-tasks or combine several sub-tasks into one task.

2 Identify resources needed

Decide what resources will be necessary to complete each task. For example, in the project of moving the company to a new building, the task of designing the new office will require an interior designer. Where these resources incur an out-of-pocket cost, this should also be noted.

3 Decide time needed

At this stage, just consider the "task time" – how long a task actually takes to complete. Use the same units of time throughout – hours, days, weeks or months as appropriate. Later you may also need to factor in "lapsed time". In the example below, seven days' task time will normally translate into nine days' lapsed time unless the designer works over weekends. (For more information on estimating time, see page 42.)

A useful way of setting up the tasks on a WBS is to divide each Post-it into three:

- Element of work (task)
- Resources required
- Task time

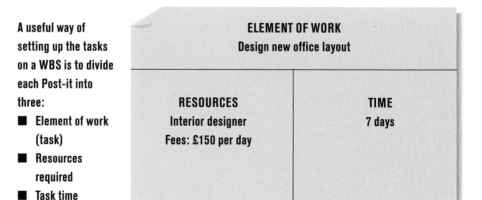

ELEMENT OF WORK Design new office layout	
RESOURCES Interior designer Fees: £150 per day	**TIME** 7 days

4 Identify dependencies

The order and timing of some tasks will be flexible. These tasks may begin simultaneously and be carried out independently of each other. For example, if the project is to decorate a room, the curtains can be made while the walls are being painted.

However, some tasks may depend on each other. There are two main types of dependency: logical dependency and resource dependency.

- Logic dependency is where one task must logically follow another. For example, the carpets cannot be laid until the painting is complete.
- Resource dependency is where two tasks cannot be carried out simultaneously. For example, if there is only one person to do the painting, the walls and the woodwork cannot be painted at the same time.

Time and dependencies

The most common link between tasks is end-start – that is, one task must end before another can start. However, you may also find the following variations.

- **Start-start**

This is when two activities must start at the same time. For example, a company about to launch a new product will generally aim to maximize the impact of their marketing activities with simultaneous PR and advertising.

- **End-end**

This is where two tasks must end at the same time. Some cooking recipes demand that several ingredients be prepared ready for combination at precisely the same moment. The skilled chef begins each activity at exactly the right moment to make this possible.

- **Staggered start**

In some cases one task can begin before its predecessor is fully complete. A farming contractor with three tractors can plough, harrow and sow a field simultaneously, thus completing the whole task in the minimum possible time. The time lag between tasks will depend on the speed of the various operations.

Estimating time in projects

Estimating the time required for tasks can be one of the most difficult parts of planning a project. A major reason for this is that time estimation techniques are based on experience, and many projects take place in unfamiliar territory.

Lapsed time

Another difficulty with estimating time is that there is often a substantial difference between "task time" and "lapsed time". To give an example, writing a magazine article might take two days, but if the author has other time commitments, it may be ten days before she can submit the article. Thus the task time is two days, but the lapsed time is ten days. Pressure from other, shorter-term deadlines and the need to coordinate the diaries of busy people are major causes of lapsed time.

Tips for estimating time

The following tips should help you estimate time accurately:

- Break down larger tasks into smaller, more manageable elements.
- Do not confuse "task time" and "lapsed time". Allocate "task time" to tasks, then work out a realistic deadline for each one.
- Use similar tasks as a yardstick for your estimates.
- Use other peoples' experience to supplement or confirm your ideas.

A FORMULA FOR ESTIMATING TIME

Suppose you have to recruit a member of staff with a specific technical skill. You have the CV of a promising candidate who could start immediately, and you are due to interview them before the end of the week. In addition, you have briefed a recruitment agency and will be advertising in a newspaper next Sunday if necessary. Your assessment for the time to recruit someone is:

Optimistic time:	1 week
Likely time:	12 weeks
Pessimistic time:	14 weeks

To come up with a reasonable time estimate, calculate:

$$\frac{\text{Optimistic time} + 4(\text{likely time}) + \text{pessimistic time}}{6}$$

$(1 + 48 + 14) \div 6 = 10.5\,\text{weeks}$

If the consequences of lateness are severe, you may need to weight the formula towards pessimism, using:

$$\frac{\text{optimistic time} + 3(\text{likely time}) + 2(\text{pessimistic time})}{6}$$

For the recruitment example, this would give
$(1 + 36 + 28) \div 6 = 10.8\,\text{weeks}$

Precedence diagrams

Once you have worked out the task times and the dependencies between tasks, you can produce a precedence diagram, which represents this information for the entire project. The strength of a precedence diagram is that it shows the links between tasks; its weakness is that the relationship between "project" time and "calendar" time is not always explicit.

The illustration below represents the tasks and dependencies in a simple precedence diagram: the project here is preparing a business presentation.

Reading the precedence diagram

You read a precedence diagram from left to right following the lines of logic along the different branches. The diagram shows the sequence of tasks, and branches occur where tasks can be carried out independently.

In the example given, the preparation of visuals and handouts cannot begin until an outline script is ready and a brief prepared. Once it is begun, however, it can proceed without depending on any other tasks. It must be completed before the rehearsal can take place.

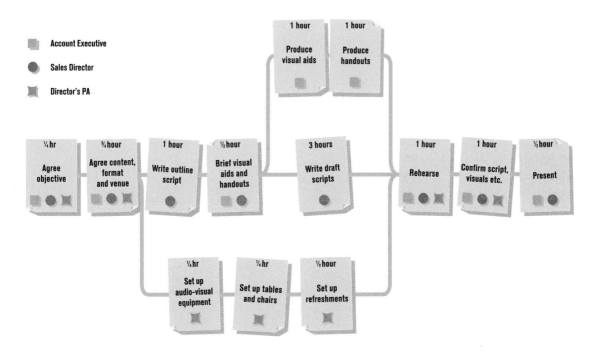

| Account Executive |
| Sales Director |
| Director's PA |

| 1 hour | 1 hour |
| Produce visual aids | Produce handouts |

| ¼ hr | ¾ hour | 1 hour | ½ hour | 3 hours | 1 hour | 1 hour | ½ hour |
| Agree objective | Agree content, format and venue | Write outline script | Brief visual aids and handouts | Write draft scripts | Rehearse | Confirm script, visuals etc. | Present |

| ¼ hr | ¼ hr | ½ hour |
| Set up audio-visual equipment | Set up tables and chairs | Set up refreshments |

Determining the critical path

When you have drawn up a precedence diagram, it is relatively easy to work out the shortest time it will take to complete the project.

Doing a "forward pass"

Starting at the left of the diagram, add together the time allowed for the first two tasks. Write the total just above the top right-hand corner of the second Post-it note. This figure is the earliest time to completion of the second task. Now move through the diagram, filling in the cumulative totals for each task.

Where paths converge, you should take the higher of the two totals preceding it. For example, the rehearsal can only take place when both the handouts and draft script are complete, so it cannot start before 5½ hours or be complete before 6½ hours.

The critical path

The tasks that add to the highest value through the whole diagram lie on what is known as the "critical path". It is the shortest time in which the project can be completed. In complex projects you may need planning software to work it out.

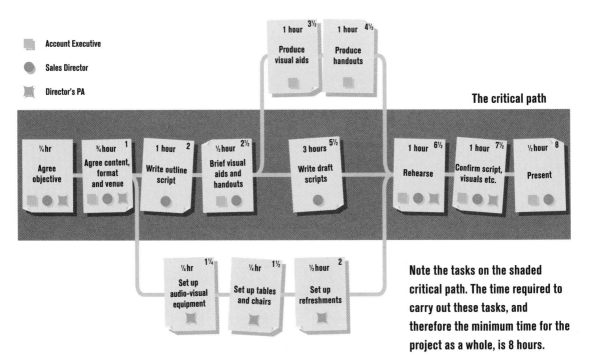

Note the tasks on the shaded critical path. The time required to carry out these tasks, and therefore the minimum time for the project as a whole, is 8 hours.

Calculating "float" time

Doing a "backward pass"

You may need to establish where there is slack time for tasks not on the critical path. To do this, write the time required for the critical path just below the bottom right-hand corner of the final task. Working backwards through the diagram, subtract task times from this figure, writing the result below each box. This figure represents the latest time by which a task must be completed.

"Float" time

For tasks not on the critical path, the number below the box (latest time for completion) is larger than the one above (earliest time for completion). The difference between the two is "float" time – how long you can delay the task without affecting the overall length of the project.

Where two paths converge, you will have two possible values to write below the box; use the smaller one. So, in the example, producing visual aids only requires the brief to be complete by 3½ hours. However, writing the draft script requires the brief to be complete by 2½ hours, so this is the figure used in calculations back through the diagram.

Where lapsed time (see page 42) is a problem, it may be impossible to identify the critical path and float times accurately – don't waste time trying to do so. Simply concentrate on tasks where delay will have maximum impact.

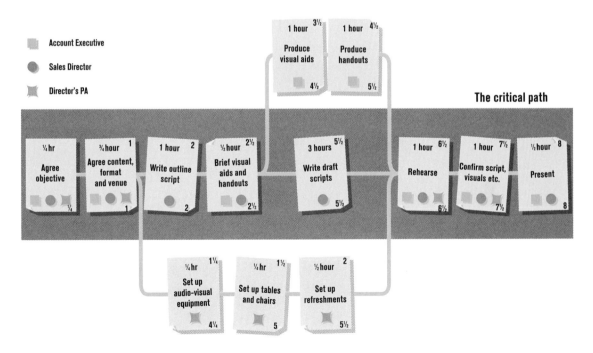

The critical path

Practical use of critical path analysis

As well as its obvious uses for scheduling, the critical path can help you decide how to allocate tasks. You need to take particular care when allocating resources to tasks on or near the critical path.

Allocating critical tasks

When allocating tasks on the critical path, or tasks that have little float time, it is often, but not always, a good idea to assign them to your most competent and committed people.

Beware the temptation to do all the critical tasks yourself. If you do this you will find it difficult to coordinate the activities of others and troubleshoot as necessary. In addition you are likely to be responsible for any slippage in the project schedule, making it extremely difficult to criticize anyone else who does not come in on time.

On occasion you may even choose to get people with negative stakes in your project involved in critical tasks as a way of reducing their ability to criticize if things go wrong.

Planning reviews

Tasks on the critical path will need to be reviewed more often than less critical tasks.

Ensure that you have at least one review of any critical task fixed in your diary far enough in advance of the absolute deadline to enable you to take any corrective action necessary. It is often useful to have an explicit escalation procedure so that you know as soon as there is a problem. So, for example, a project manager might agree with a team member that he should not accept extra commitments in a given week without consulting her.

Treat float time as an opportunity

You can use tasks with float as opportunities to coach people in new skills. People are often drawn to project work by the chance it offers for self-development. Do not be afraid to have inexperienced people doing tasks that are a long way from the critical path.

Review the critical path

The project manager needs to check progress against the critical path periodically, because during the life of a project, the critical path can change. There is also a danger of concentrating exclusively on tasks on the critical path. Other tasks of similar duration going on at the same time may be just as important.

Risk

Any project plan should take account of the possibility that things may go wrong, and set up procedures to deal with this. Assessing and planning for risk is therefore an important responsibility of the project manager at the planning stage.

Types of risk

The risks involved in a project may arise from a number of factors. However, the project manager need only be concerned with risks affecting any of the three project parameters of Time, Cost and Quality.

POSSIBLE SOURCES OF RISK

- **PEOPLE**
  Are they available?
  Are they committed?
  Are they skilled?
  Do they know what is required of them?

- **TECHNICAL**
  Is the technology proven?
  Is it reliable?
  Is it available?
  Is it understood?

- **POLITICAL**
  Is the need for the project agreed?
  Does the sponsor control the stakeholder group?
  Are negative stakeholders influential?
  Is communication with stakeholders good?

- **FINANCIAL**
  Am I in control of project funds?

- **CONTRACTUAL/LEGAL**
  Am I, or my company, contractually or legally liable for the failure of any element of the project?

- **PHYSICAL**
  Are there any physical risks inherent in undertaking project tasks?

- **ENVIRONMENTAL**
  How can the weather affect my project?
  What geological factors might put the project's success at risk?

Risk

Assessing the risks

There are two factors to take into account when assessing risks.

■ How likely is it to happen?

■ How serious will it be if it does?

In each case, you should aim to rate the risk on a scale of one to ten. For instance, if you were assessing the risk of a labour dispute, you might decide it was fairly unlikely (3), but that the results would be very serious (9). You then multiply your two figures together, which will give you a figure between one and 100. The higher the figure, the more seriously you need to treat the risk.

Planning for risk

Just about every task in your project will contain some element of risk. What the project manager has to do is decide at what level the risk should be regarded as serious.

A typical recommendation is that you use 25 on the risk assessment scale (medium likelihood × medium seriousness) as your cut-off point. Any task with a risk rating above that needs to be looked at in advance, and progress towards its completion monitored more carefully than usual. You may also need to have a backup plan for the most serious risks.

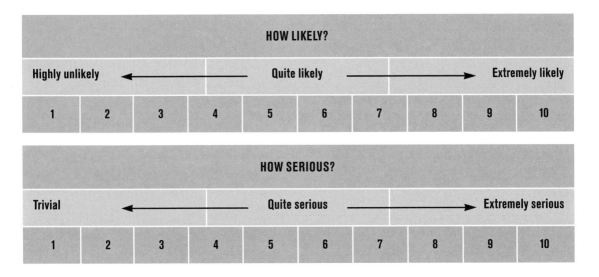

Recording risk

Once you have identified tasks where the risk is higher than average, you may find it helpful to record them in a risk register, using a format like the one given below. This approach encourages you to anticipate what might otherwise come as a complete surprise.

In many cases you will have to search actively for early indications of problems. For instance, if you have delegated recruitment of 400 market research interviewees within five days, a warning sign would be if only 20 have been recruited by the end of the first day. You will only know this if you request daily updates on progress.

Dealing with risk

In order to make the effort of planning for risk worthwhile, you need to be able to do something about it when a risk has been identified. There are three main ways of dealing with risk.

■ **Avoid**

Identify the cause of the risk and try to avoid it. In the example given, you might recognize that recruiting 400 interviewees within five days will be impossible, and plan the research to take account of a smaller sample.

■ **Deflect**

See if you can get others to underwrite or take on some of the risk so that you do not bear the consequences alone. You might make the client responsible for recruiting their own interviewees.

■ **Make a contingency plan**

Have a backup plan that will allow your plans to stay largely intact. You might increase the number of people involved in recruitment, change the database from which you are recruiting, or broaden the parameters of the sample.

SAMPLE RISK REGISTER					
Task	What could go wrong	Risk assessment (1 – 100)	Parameter affected (T/C/Q)	Early indicators	Action
Recruit interviewees	Can't recruit 400 in time?	15	Time	Less than 80 at end of day one.	Broaden parameters; use smaller sample.

Team planning

The planning activities discussed so far can be carried out by the team rather than by the project manager alone.

Planning as a team

Where there are several people involved, planning is best carried out along the lines of a brainstorming session. Like a brainstorming session, a team planning meeting should have three stages: the creative phase, in which the team generates as many ideas as possible; the evaluation phase, in which the merits of the ideas are assessed and the best ideas selected; and the planning phase, in which the team decide how to put the ideas into action.

Facilitator

The facilitator has prime responsibility for the brainstorming process. The project manager often takes this role.

The facilitator should start by ensuring that the objective and scope of the project is understood by all.

Next, they must maintain the discipline of postponing judgement of ideas until the creative phase of the meeting is complete.

During the evaluation phase, the facilitator should concentrate on ensuring that everyone has an opportunity to input ideas and air concerns. Finally, in the planning phase, they should prompt the group to commit to specific actions, timescales and responsibilities.

The problem owner

Ideally the role of problem owner should be played by the client or end user. Failing this, it may be a good way of involving the sponsor. The problem owner is responsible for focusing the group on any specific problems that need to be resolved and identifying the value in ideas they come up with.

The problem owner gives a summary outline of the objective, then takes a back seat while brainstorming takes place, intervening with further clarification of the problem only if the creative session is going off-course. At the end of the creative phase, they are responsible for choosing the ideas that have greatest merit.

Resources

Everyone else in the meeting acts as resources. Their function is to generate a volume of ideas. If the facilitator and problem owner are doing their jobs, people will enjoy acting as resources.

Ideally these resources will be members of the team who will then work on the project, though this may not turn out to be the case.

Representing a project plan

There are various ways to represent your plans on paper (or on a computer). Specialist project management software usually offers a wide range of options, some of them specifically designed to help identify and monitor different aspects of the project. A precedence diagram is a useful way of representing the work flow for the entire project. Two other types of representation that project managers find useful are Gantt charts and histograms.

Gantt charts

A Gantt chart shows the duration of tasks within the timescale for the entire project. The horizontal axis is the time line; tasks are listed vertically, with each task's timing and duration represented by a horizontal line or band.

The advantage of the Gantt chart is that the broad phases of the project are immediately obvious, with real-time dates for every event. It also makes it easy for the project team to monitor progress against the original plan.

Gantt chart

ACTIVITY	Wk 1	Wk 2	Wk 3	Wk 4	Wk 5	Wk 6	Wk 7	Wk 8	Wk 9	Wk 10	Wk 11	Wk 12	Wk 13	Wk 14	Wk 15
Proof read material	▓	▓	▓	▓	▓										
Prepare marketing plan for product		▓	▓	▓	▓	▓	▓								
Set up Launch					▓	▓									
Attend Launch												▓			
Write Marketing Report													▓	▓	▓
Prepare Plan for Product 2															

Representing a project plan

Histograms

A histogram is simply a fancy name for a bar chart. Histograms can be used to show the resources in use at different stages of the project and alert the project manager to points where resource demand will be greater than the pool available.

In the chart shown here, if you have only five engineers available in your internal team, you may either have to bring in additional resources in weeks 4, 5, 7 and 9, or increase the length of the project to allow the additional work

to be done by the internal engineers. The value of recognizing problems of this kind in the planning phase should not be underestimated.

Choosing representations

The project manager has the right to choose which of these representations best suits their purposes. As a rule, most people find that the precedence diagram is of most use in creating the plan; once this is done, the Gantt chart format makes it easiest to track progress as the project proceeds.

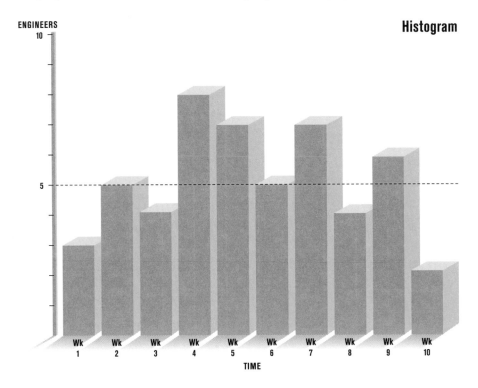

Histogram

ENGINEERS

TIME

Software

Purpose-built computer software packages are available to help project managers plan and coordinate projects. If your project is too complex to plan and coordinate manually, you will almost certainly find a package to suit you.

Do you really need it?

Project software is no more than a vehicle to carry your project plan. If your plan is relatively simple, the demands of the software may be out of all proportion to the benefits you can derive from using it. You may even find that instead of making your job easier, the software is creating extra work.

Computerized diary systems

If you are running a project substantially on your own and with a relatively simple budget, an electronic diary system may suit your scheduling needs. These now come as standard with many major office software packages. They can schedule tasks for particular times or days, post reminders for you and others, and allow you to monitor progress.

If you and your project team are all on the same computer network, you can have access to each other's diaries, making it easy to coordinate meetings and monitor activity.

Spreadsheet applications

A standard spreadsheet application may be able to generate graphs showing budgeted and actual cost and time usage with far less fuss than specialist software. The advantage of a standard package is that you can decide how much or how little detail to include. In addition, if you are already familiar with the programme you will not have to spend time learning a new system.

Specialist project software

If you are certain that you need specialist software, decide in advance what you need, then look for the programme that will deliver this. Do not design your specification around what the programme can do. If you do, features that you do not really need may seem essential as soon as you are aware that they exist.

DECIDING WHAT YOU WANT
Some questions that may help you clarify what you need are:
- How many people need access to the software?
- What software are they already used to?
- How much additional training will they need?
- What package can be supported in my I.T. environment?
- What reports do I need?
- How do I want to display my plan?
- How much is my budget?

Planning checklist

1 Briefly restate the scope and objectives of the project.

2 Brainstorm the project deliverables. Create a Deliverable Breakdown Structure (DBS).

3 Brainstorm the tasks required to complete each deliverable. Create a Work Breakdown Structure (WBS).

4 Allocate times to tasks (remember these are "task times" at this point).

5 Work out an initial order of tasks.

6 Identify logical dependencies.

7 Identify gaps.

8 Allocate responsibilities.

9 Identify resource dependencies. Confirm all dependencies.

10 Where "task time" and "lapsed time" are the same, do a forward pass along all dependency paths to identify the shortest possible start to finish time – the critical path.

11 Do a backward pass through the diagram to identify float time.

12 Conduct a detailed risk assessment.

Even when you have completed all the steps listed here, remember that things will change and some assumptions will prove incorrect, so planning remains a key responsibility of the project manager throughout the implementation phase.

Planning glossary

Deliverable
The product of all or part of the project.

Deliverable breakdown structure (DBS)
A complete list of all the things a project needs to produce (deliverables) in order to achieve its objective, grouped in a logical hierarchy.

Work breakdown structure (WBS)
All the tasks that need to be done to produce the deliverables. In its most unstructured form a WBS is a list of all tasks. In larger projects it may be broken down hierarchically into one or more levels of sub-tasks.

Dependency
The relationship between two tasks. The most common dependency is where one task must be completed before another can be started.

Precedence (or Network) diagram
A method of representing a project plan using boxes to represent activities and lines to represent relationships between them.

Gantt chart
A bar chart using time as its horizontal axis and in which the durations of tasks are represented geometrically.

Histogram
Bar chart representing levels of resource required at various stages of the project.

Task
A unit of work requiring action by an individual or group to achieve a defined result. It may consist of several sub-tasks or activities.

Sub-task (or Activity)
A single activity or unit of work that generally needs to be completed in one go and requires an individual or group for its entire duration.

Milestone (or Checkpoint)
A fixed date or time in a project, usually associated with a progress review.

Float time
The amount of time that a task can afford to slip by without having an effect on overall project timings.

Critical path
The sequence of tasks whose durations added together define the shortest possible length of the project.

Critical path analysis
The process of identifying the shortest route through the project and the amount of float on non-critical tasks.

4

Manage your team
Delegate wherever possible
Review progress frequently
Make it happen

How can I keep everybody happy?
Can somebody else do this?
Who needs to know about changes?

Working on your own

Often the challenge when working on your own is to find enough "quality" time to make progress with project tasks when your diary is already full coping with the short-term deadlines that inevitably crop up on a daily basis.

Set a daily project goal

Make sure that you take at least one step towards your project goal every day, no matter how small.

Make time

Create regular slots of "project time". It can be scheduled into your diary two or three times a week like a meeting. Ideally sessions should be about two hours in length and booked several weeks in advance.

Anticipate obstacles

Try to book a quiet venue where you can work uninterrupted. Spend ten minutes a couple of days ahead of each period of "project time" identifying the information you need and taking action to ensure it will be available when you need it.

To minimize the disruption your absence might cause, you may need to get a colleague to answer your phone and field any interruptions. Book some "call back" time at the end of "project time" so that you can guarantee being available to speak to people and return their phone calls.

Appoint a conscience

Find someone to act as the voice of your conscience. Pick someone who is not afraid to bully you if necessary and ask them to check on your progress at regular intervals. If you have a designated project sponsor this is a role that they will fill.

MAKE SURE YOU MAKE PROGRESS

■ Set a daily project goal

■ Schedule project time into your diary

■ Get a colleague to cover for you

■ Ask someone to bully you

Managing a project team

Ultimately, an effective project manager is one who achieves the required result. If your projects involve a number of people, success will rely as much on your people skills – your ability to build teams, delegate tasks and motivate others – as on any specialized technical abilities you might have to offer.

A balancing act

The project manager's role as team leader is well described in John Adair's book *Functional Model of Leadership*. His research indicates that successful managers are those who are able to balance the needs of:

- the task – achieving a result
- the individual – providing clear goals, motivation and feedback
- the team – facilitating communication and giving the team a sense of identity

Adair emphasizes the point that while a leader must fulfil all three functions, some of their activities will have an impact in more than one area. For example, by setting goals for individual team members, the project manager can increase the likelihood of a successful outcome to the task, motivate the individual and define roles within the team.

Conversely, concentrating on one area to the detriment of others could ultimately threaten the success of the project as a whole.

Leadership through a project

In the different phases of a project, leadership tasks will be different. The chart on the following two pages offers suggestions for the activities the project manager might consider during each phase under the headings of task, team and individual functions.

"Agree roles and responsibilities"

Managing a project team

PHASE	TASK
DEFINITION	■ Define scope – meet/talk to client and sponsor. Deliverable: definition document.
PLANNING	■ Plan tasks, deliverables, risks, milestones, dependencies, expenditure and responsibilities Deliverable: project schedule and budget.
IMPLEMENTATION	■ Monitor progress against project schedule/budget. ■ Modify the plan as necessary. ■ Identify and record changes to scope. ■ Liaise with sponsor and client. Deliverable: project deliverables.
HANDOVER	■ Confirm objectives met. ■ Hold official handover event. ■ Produce end-user instructions. Deliverable: completed project.
REVIEW	■ Conduct post-project review. Agree learning points. Deliverable: project review document (published in an appropriate format).

TEAM	INDIVIDUAL
■ Name the project – This will give the team a point of reference as it forms. ■ Negotiate a "team building" budget.	■ Identify the people you would like to take part. Take preliminary soundings on availability and interest. ■ Assemble the "planning team".
■ Hold preliminary team meeting(s) to establish roles and ground rules. ■ Produce project "organization chart". ■ Set up a group diary and e-mail address group. ■ Agree dates for review meetings.	■ Select individuals. ■ Delegate tasks. ■ Identify skills shortfalls and agree personal development goals. ■ Open a "personal" file on each team member.
■ Communicate progress to all team members. ■ Maintain the profile of the project via minutes, articles and briefings. ■ Resolve disputes if they arise. ■ Integrate new team members. ■ Arrange regular social events.	■ Monitor initial delegation. ■ Delegate further tasks. ■ Bring in new people as required. ■ Coach individuals. ■ Hold individual review meetings. ■ Maintain an appropriate level of individual social contact.
■ Involve the team in handover. ■ Represent team in success or failure. ■ Pass on feedback and rewards to team.	■ Debrief individual performances. Agree any feedback that will be passed to manager. ■ Reward success. ■ Thank individuals.
■ Combine the post-project review with a social event to say thank-you to all participants.	■ Write reports on individuals noting any skills learnt/experience gained with recommendations for the future.

Delegation

For any manager, delegation is a critical skill. It is particularly challenging in the context of a project where work groups are temporary and lines of authority are less clearly defined.

A project manager may also face the challenges that he or she may be junior to some of the team members and that, because project work is rarely urgent, it may get less attention than other tasks with more pressing deadlines. Delegation requests must be clearly defined and persuasively presented if they are to be accepted by colleagues already busy with other things.

Delegate early

Wherever possible, plan delegation well in advance, and delegate early. Three weeks' warning of a deadline is nearly always preferable to three days'. A detailed project plan should be your first reference when delegating, but in addition set time aside regularly throughout the project to plan what, how, and to whom you will delegate.

As soon as you are aware that you would like to delegate you might consider giving the delegatee a warning to that effect, outlining the scope and arranging a meeting at which the formal delegation will take place.

BENEFITS OF DELEGATION		
For the organization	For the project manager (delegator)	For the project team member (delegatee)
■ Allows fullest use of available resources. ■ Encourages broadest spread of expertise. ■ Develops highest level of teamwork and morale.	■ Frees up time to gain an overview of progress. ■ Ensures highest quality results. ■ Allows work to be done quicker through concurrent activity.	■ Gives opportunity to learn or practice new skills. ■ Enables them to work on more important aspects of company business. ■ Exposes them to new and challenging situations.

The delegation meeting

Prepare thoroughly for the delegation meeting. Have all the supporting information you need with you. In particular, remember your diary.

At the meeting, ensure that the person you are giving a task or responsibility to understands exactly what you expect of them and is committed to carrying out the task. You will need to explain, and perhaps demonstrate, what you require and by when. They should be given an opportunity to ask questions, raise any concerns and negotiate on time, cost and quality. You may also need to coach them in a new skill – you should make sure they understand that you are prepared to do so. All these activities take time but should be seen as an investment that invariably pays off in the long run.

BLOCKS ON DELEGATION

Many project managers freely admit that they do not delegate as much as they should. This is usually either because they have a negative attitude to delegation or because they are simply unaware of how and when to do it. If you find it difficult to delegate, you may end up overloaded with tasks while your team members become discontented because they are not entrusted with more responsibility, so it is important to recognize what is stopping you. The following factors are among the most common blocks to delegation.

FEAR
- of losing control
- of upsetting subordinates
- of failure
- of being outshone by able subordinates

GUILT
- at not delegating soon enough
- at passing on unpleasant tasks

OVER-ENTHUSIASM
- We sometimes continue to do tasks we should delegate because we enjoy them

INSECURITY
- People who fear for their own positions often refuse to delegate for fear that they will become dispensable

POWERLESSNESS
- The mistaken belief that there is no-one to delegate to. Powerlessness is first and foremost a state of mind

LACK OF ASSERTIVENESS
- Inexperienced managers sometimes overlook opportunities to delegate that require them to be assertive

Delegation

A good way of ensuring understanding and commitment is to delegate in two parts with a period of "thinking" time in between.

1 Brief the delegatee.

2 Ask for feedback. The delegatee briefs you on their understanding of the goal and the method they will use to achieve it.

Agree and stick to review dates

A delegation meeting should never end without agreement on the deadline and at least one review session written into both your diaries. Often you will be in a position to set up a framework of reviews that provide an opportunity to:

■ keep abreast of progress, redirecting progress if necessary
■ pool the best new ideas
■ give praise and recognition
■ maintain focus on the job at hand

Even if the delegatee seems likely to cope well, you should add contingency time into your plan . Agree a final review in advance of the ultimate deadline to give some "buffer time" for last-minute corrections.

Delegate jobs with a tangible result

People are more motivated when they can say "I did that!" Look for opportunities to delegate whole jobs. This may mean that you have to coach the delegatee or give them increased levels of authority.

Don't hover

Be available for help when you are needed, but resist the temptation to hover over the person doing the task, watching their every move. You have delegated to this person because you trust them to do the job and to save you time. Hovering over them will annoy them and you might as well be doing the job yourself.

Most people hover because they fear they will lose track of their delegation. Establishing the review meetings mentioned above can easily cure this.

On completion

Accept what has been produced as long as it fulfils the intended result and don't "nit pick!"

Ensure that any final feedback you give is specific and actionable. Praise in public; criticize in private.

Style

The style in which you delegate depends largely on the competence and commitment of the delegatee. The more competent and committed they are, the less controlling your style needs to be. By delegating the maximum level of authority you empower the delegatee to act on their own initiative.

Choose the most appropriate style

The most appropriate style will give the highest quality results in the most time-efficient manner. In order to choose a style, consider the following:

■ How competent is the delegatee for the task to be undertaken?

■ What stake has the delegatee in the success of the task to be delegated or the project overall?

■ How much initiative is the delegatee being asked to display in other areas of their life? (Someone who is already having to take a lot of initiative elsewhere may welcome being told what to do.)

Do not assume anything. If in doubt, ask.

STYLES OF DELEGATION				
1. DO AS I SAY	**2. ASK MY PERMISSION**	**3. ASK MY ADVICE**	**4. TELL ME WHAT YOU'VE DONE**	**5. HAVE MY JOB!**
Use when you need immediate action or when explaining a fixed process that must be followed.	As delegator you retain control but expect the delegatee to come to you with ideas.	You pass control to the delegatee, but retain a close interest in what he/she proposes to do.	You have enough confidence in the delegatee to allow him/her to brief you retrospectively.	The ultimate aim of the true delegator is to prepare the delegatee to take over. Recognition that you are prepared to move to level 5 can often be a powerful motivator to the delegatee and is the mark of a good manager.

Communications within projects

The project manager has a vital role as the facilitator of communications both within the team and between the project and the wider group of stakeholders. This is particularly true in the implementation phase of a project.

■ Draw up a project team organization and stakeholder chart during the planning phase. Remember to include the external team in your reckoning. Review this at intervals during implementation.

■ Take time at any initial team building session to agree the frequency and format of communications that will take place within your team. If you do not have a team, remember that you should still agree how you will communicate with your sponsor.

■ Where appropriate, discuss and agree what information your main stakeholders – in particular any end users – need.

■ Minute any decisions or understandings in writing for future reference.

■ Set up e-mail address groups for your project team and stakeholders.

Active listening

A skilled communicator can see the world through the eyes of the person they are communicating with. This perspective can only be gained if you ask appropriate questions and take time to listen.

Open questions will help you to ascertain people's views, and summarizing their answers accurately will show that you have understood even if you do not agree with them.

OPEN QUESTIONS
Questions which encourage full answers are open questions. For example:

■ What is your opinion about this project?

■ Why do you want to outsource this part of the project?

■ How will you and your team keep on track during the final phase?

■ Where do you see your priorities lying in the next three weeks?

■ When do you anticipate this task being completed?

Match the medium to the message

Communication can take a variety of forms, each suitable for different circumstances. When deciding on the best way of getting your message across two of the most important factors to consider are logic and emotion. Ask yourself these questions.

- How difficult is the message to understand?
- Are there any negative implications of the message? Do I need to motivate this person to take action?

How do we communicate?

Research has shown that we derive about 60 percent of communication from body language, about 30 percent from our tone of voice and a mere 10 percent from the words we use.

This means that we are at our most effective communicating face-to-face. However, this is not always practical, and in any case you have to balance your need to communicate effectively with the need to make effective use of time – both yours and your colleagues'.

SELECTING THE BEST METHOD OF COMMUNICATION			
HIGH LOGICAL COMPLEXITY		**LOW LOGICAL COMPLEXITY**	
LOW EMOTIONAL COMPLEXITY	**HIGH EMOTIONAL COMPLEXITY**	**LOW EMOTIONAL COMLEXITY**	**HIGH EMOTIONAL COMPLEXITY**
Example: "Here is my complete client database"	Example: "We want these three changes made to the scope of the project"	Example: "Can I have another copy of that document"	Example: "The project will not be ready on time…"
Suggestion: Put it in writing. If the information is needed fast, use fax or e-mail.	Suggestion: Deliver this message face-to-face. The recipient will no doubt want to ask questions. Arrange a formal meeting.	Suggestion: E-mail would be ideal for this, or the telephone. Do not waste time with a face-to-face interruption unless the request is urgent.	Suggestion: Best done face-to-face or occasionally on the phone. If it is required in writing, precede with an ad hoc meeting or phone call.

Project review meetings

A project should start with a definition meeting and end with a project learning review meeting. In addition, there should also be interim review meetings.

Regardless of what they are called, review meetings are an essential tool for monitoring progress and allocating future tasks within the team. Yet review meetings are often anticipated with dread and end up being a complete waste of time. Almost invariably this is due to a lack of preparation either by the chairperson or by delegates.

Before the meeting

Preparation is vital both for the chairperson and the delegates. If you are chairperson, half an hour's preparatory thought will usually enable you to define the objective of the meeting, and what is expected of each delegate. You can then decide how long you need, what facilities are required and who needs to be there.

Make sure that all those taking part are told well in advance what they are expected to contribute. Be as specific as possible. Do not fall into the trap of holding a meeting with a "standard" set of headings. This will only evoke a "standard" set of excuses! Have an agenda that follows a logical sequence.

SAMPLE DRAFT AGENDA

Invitees _____

Venue _____

Date _____

Time _____
Start _____
End _____
PURPOSE _____

ITEM 1
Title _____
Purpose _____
Preparation _____
Outcome _____
Responsible _____
Time _____

ITEM 2 _____
Title etc. _____

Draft agenda

Two or three weeks before the meeting, send out a draft agenda with all relevant information. Invite comments to be returned to the chairperson by five days prior to the meeting.

Final agenda

Two to five days before the meeting, send out the final agenda incorporating all changes to the draft and confirming timings and attendance lists.

At the meeting

Always try to start your meetings on time. This is not only good manners to those who have made the effort to attend; it also sets a professional tone for the rest of the proceedings. State the purpose of the meeting and the purpose of each item. Keep an eye on the time and keep things moving.

Do not allow waffle or deviation and be quick to stamp on personal attacks. However, do not be afraid to confront poor performance or unacceptable behaviour.

Summarize what has been said to ensure that you, and everyone else, have understood it. Record action points so that you have something to refer back to in case of any misunderstandings. Make sure they are allocated to a person at the meeting

and that a deadline is set prior to the next meeting. Ensure you note this in your diary so that you can follow it up.

After the meeting

Produce minutes in good time. You may find it useful to get "Action Minutes" out within 24 hours of the meeting. This a brief resumé of work that needs to be carried out.

Action minutes can be followed by a fuller record of proceedings, produced within about a week, if necessary. Do not allow minutes to wait until the next review meeting before they become public. Working on the principle that most people complete their actions either immediately after being given them or just before the deadline, you may find it useful to circulate a further copy of the minutes with the draft agenda for the next review meeting.

Where appropriate, follow action points up personally to ensure they are being carried out. This may be done in a series of one-to-one reviews with individual members of your team.

CHECKLIST FOR REVIEW MEETINGS
- ■ Prepare
- ■ Inform
- ■ Control
- ■ Record
- ■ Minute

Project records

Much of the information for project records may be kept electronically, which has the advantage of reducing volume and increasing availability to the whole team.

As project manager you may be responsible for large amounts of information relating to work in progress. The trick is never to have superfluous paperwork cluttering your working area, but always to have the right information to hand.

In some organizations a quality system lays down exactly what information needs to be stored and how. If your organization does not have these procedures laid down, the following guidelines may be of help.

KEY RECORDS

Regardless of the scale of your project, keep a record of the following:
- definition document
- stakeholder chart
- team organization chart
- communications chart
- project plan
- risk register

In addition you are likely to have:
- minutes of all review meetings
- change records
- personal files on team members

MAINTAINING PROJECT RECORDS

- Create a project folder or filing system with a checklist of records that it should contain.
- Use colour coded paper to make it easy to identify documents at a glance.
- Weed files of out-of-date information once a month.
- Note the version numbers of any document that is frequently revised or updated.
- Separate "Archive" information (for example, back copies of documents) that is being kept pending a final review from "Reference" information (such as the project plan) that is in regular use. This makes it easier to find what you are looking for quickly.
- File "Active" documents (those requiring a specific future action) in date order using a "Bring Forward" file.

Changing the project scope

A successful project is founded on a clear definition and a robust plan. While the plan may change to overcome unforeseen problems, changes to the scope should be rare. However, sometimes it is necessary or desirable to re-scope a project.

Put it in writing

Changes to the scope of the project should always be agreed in writing with the project sponsor. By creating written records, you ensure that no misunderstanding can exist between you, and encourage detailed thought about the impact on time and resources.

The framework given here covers the items that should be considered when making changes to time, cost and quality. The format may seem a bit formal in some circumstances, in which case you may prefer to minute your agreement of these points in the form of a letter, e-mail or memo that is then sent to the sponsor.

The same techniques that were used to draw up the original scope should be used to make any changes.

Ensure that all those affected by changes are informed immediately. Remember, if the change is likely to generate any negative reaction, it may be necessary to talk it through face to face or on the phone.

CHANGE REQUEST PROFORMA

■ **SPECIFIC CHANGE REQUESTED**

REQUESTED BY

■ **REASON FOR CHANGE**

■ **METHOD TO BE ADOPTED**

PEOPLE AFFECTED

■ **EFFECTS ON:**
a. **QUALITY**
1) **Essential features affected?**

2) **Desirable features affected?**

b. **TIME**

c. **COST/RESOURCES**

■ **ADDITIONAL INFORMATION**

■ **DECLARATION OF AGREEMENT**
PROJECT SPONSOR

PROJECT MANAGER

Ensure you are not trading off an essential feature to gain one that is merely desirable.

5

Engage stakeholders early
Clarify expectations
Brief end users
Celebrate success

Who is the handover for?
When does handover take place?
How do I plan for it?

Project handover

Handover marks the point at which the project team's responsibility for development ends and the end user is fully capable of taking on whatever the project produced. Purely at a practical level this requires certain adjustments by both parties. However, there is also an important psychological element in handover that project managers ignore at their peril.

Significance to the project team

Without a clearly defined point of handover, project workers can drift off into a kind of limbo and find it difficult to move on. Often they feel dissatisfied that their efforts have not been recognized, let alone rewarded.

Sometimes, particularly in large and complex projects, workers are unsure exactly what has been achieved until they see it handed over to the end user.

Finally, there is a real danger that, unless the point of handover is clearly marked, project workers will find their future productivity hampered by requests for support from end users that should properly be referred elsewhere.

Significance to the end user

For the end user, handover is the point at which they should take responsibility for what has been produced. This will normally mean a change in the way they operate, which in turn may demand new skills or impose new responsibilities. Even when they recognize the long-term benefits, people tend to react negatively to any change imposed on them without explanation. Handover activities are designed to make end users aware of what they can expect and to give them the support they need to make the transitions required.

Handover activities

Although logically the handover phase comes between implementation and review in the project sequence, success depends on a continuous stream of activities that begin in the definition phase and are planned into the implementation phase. Management experts W. Chan Kim and René Mauborgne have identified three categories of handover activity: engagement, explanation and expectation clarity.

CATEGORY	WHAT IS IT?	TYPICAL ACTIVITIES
ENGAGEMENT	Involving stakeholders, particularly end users, in change early on to lay the foundations of a successful handover. Most people enjoy being involved in change; they tend to react negatively if they suddenly find it is being done to them. Engagement activities typically take place in the definition phase.	■ holding a "selling" event under the auspices of the project sponsor ■ conducting research to canvass ideas ■ creating a prototype for people to comment on ■ listening to any concerns and incorporating improvements
EXPLANATION	Explanation should take the form of a continuous dialogue between the project team and the end user throughout the implementation phase. The end user should be told what they will be getting, when, and with what support. The benefits of the project should be emphasized and any negative effects recognized. Changes to the scope of the project should be communicated to end users as soon as they occur.	■ circulation of the final definition document ■ circulation of any change documents ■ circulation of progress reports coming out of project review meetings ■ management briefings ■ roadshows ■ poster campaigns ■ intranet briefings
EXPECTATION CLARITY	People want to know what changes they can expect when the project is complete, and to feel confident that they will have the support they need. Timing is important – if this information is given too early it will be forgotten. You will probably have to to reinforce the message several times before it is remembered by all stakeholders	■ launch events ■ training for end users ■ a "help desk" ■ step-by-step guides

Case study 1: unsuccessful handover

Failure to engage stakeholders can damage even the most carefully planned and worthwhile project.

The project

The new sales director decided that, in response to the increased sales target he had been given, all his executives should have interpersonal skills training. He made it his top priority to select and brief a well-known sales training company, investing a significant sum of money in five three-day workshops to run by the end of the first quarter. He immediately circulated dates, giving people about two months' notice of the courses.

A lack of engagement

One week later the sales director noted that people were not putting their names down and sent an e-mail reminding them of the increased targets and telling them to select their preferred dates. When, one week later, the situation had not changed he simply allocated people to courses.

The result

In order to emphasize the importance that he attached to the initiative, the sales director decided that he would attend the first programme himself. Despite this, four of twelve delegates did not turn up for the programme, and those who did attend spent much of their time questioning the relevance of the training.

At the end of the first programme, the sales training company recommended postponing further courses until they had conducted a proper "needs assessment". The sales director accepted reluctantly that this was necessary, even though it meant a postponement fee levied on the next four programmes and a delay of two months on any further training – all this in addition to the time and money wasted on the first programme.

ANALYSIS

Because of inadequate consultation early in the process of setting up the courses, people interpreted the training as an insult to their ability and did not buy into it. The tragedy was that the needs uncovered by the training company when consulting the sales force were substantially those covered by the original programme. A well-designed project to meet a real need foundered because of failure to engage stakeholders in the planning phase.

Case study 2: successful handover

The project

The IT/office manager of a medium-sized PR agency was tasked to look for ways of using technology to reduce the size of his team in order to make it possible to develop a library and research function without increasing staff numbers overall.

His first move was to call a meeting of his team where he explained what was being asked of him and invited suggestions for areas to investigate. During the meeting, he suggested they might look at replacing the telephone exchange, currently run on a rota basis by three people, with a more modern one that could be run by fewer people. Not unnaturally the switchboard operators were quick to see the danger to their jobs in this suggestion.

Engaging the stakeholders

Over the next two months, the manager invited several companies to come in and explain their systems, ensuring that at least one and sometimes two of the telephonists were involved in every meeting. At the end of the process he asked them which of the systems offered the best value for money.

The result

To his surprise, the telephonists unanimously suggested one that abolished the need for dedicated switchboard operators completely. When he pointed out that this would mean an end to their role, he found that two of the three were prepared to take voluntary redundancy and the other had identified another position within the company that she was interested in. After further investigation she was retained and continued to contribute in her new role.

ANALYSIS
By involving the telephonists at every stage, the office manager made it difficult for them to oppose a plan that made such obvious business sense. Even if there had been no other opportunities available, no one could have complained that they had been unfairly treated.

If handover is carried out successfully, end users will feel ownership even of the more unwelcome changes the project brings.

Handover checklist

To make the handover of your project a success you should consider some or all of the following activities in the various phases of the project.

1 Definition phase

- Produce a model or prototype of the end product for your end users.
- Agree when they should expect to get it.
- Explain the reasons for the project and the benefits of its product.
- Explain, as far as you are able, the impact the product will have on them (warts and all!).

The way you communicate these things to your end user will depend on the size of the project. For a small-scale project within your own company, it might be a matter of sitting at someone's desk and sketching out your proposal on the back of an envelope. At other end of the scale, you might decide to run a "roadshow" which in itself could be quite a complex event requiring careful planning.

2 Planning phase

- Incorporate time and budget in your plan for handover activities.
- Plan progress reviews with interested stakeholders.
- Set a target date for a launch event(s).
- Bid for any facilities and equipment needed.
- Warn people to set aside time for the event.

In a long-running project, your target date may not be more exact than the year in which you anticipate completion. This is acceptable as long as you tighten up on timings as soon as possible during implementation. Equally, you may be involved in a project that will end with a phased "roll out", where handover takes place over months, or even years. This situation contains potential for confusion, so ensure that people are clear exactly what to expect and by when, and think carefully about your communication plan. Simple messages are usually best.

3 Implementation phase

- Inform stakeholders of any changes to the original product or launch date as soon as possible.
- Spend time listening to your stakeholders' hopes and concerns for your project.
- Address any change management issues that the product will create. For example, find out what help people need to react positively to the product.
- Take time to plan and rehearse the details of any handover event.

Take every opportunity to confirm people's understanding of what you are doing – you will be amazed at how quickly people forget what your project is about and either dismiss or overplay its significance. The project manager needs to manage stakeholders' expectations throughout the implementation phase using every means of communication available.

Avoid seeming to take yourself too seriously, but beware undermining your project's credibility by flippant or cynical assessments of its chances of success.

4 Handover phase

- Test what you have produced. Involve the sponsor and end users.
- Produce supporting documentation and carry out trials to make sure it is adequate.
- Produce and trial any training needed to allow end users to interpret and operate the results.
- Plan the handover event(s).
- Rehearse the handover event(s).
- Hold a celebratory event for the project team.
- Reassign project personnel.
- Reassign or dispose of any project equipment, materials and supplies.
- Activate any "help desk" arrangement that will provide ongoing support for the end user following your project.

However successful your project has been in objective terms, the way people view its success will be greatly influenced by the way the handover is handled. Remember, too, that handover is for two audiences: the end users and the project team. Ensure that you take account of the needs of both groups.

Even if handover will take place by degrees, always consider how you wish to present the results of your work. First impressions are powerful and a little stage management can go a long way.

Celebrating success

Top sporting events usually end with the presentation of a trophy. Watching the emotion displayed at the moment of presentation, you could be forgiven for thinking that the trophy is more important than the actual winning – even when the prize has little intrinsic value or has to be given back afterwards.

If you have managed a team that has achieved a successful result in a project, consider how you might celebrate and recognize that success. Even in projects that have had only moderate success, where mistakes have been made and lessons learned (and that is the majority of projects!) there will still be things to celebrate. If you miss the opportunity to do so, you and your team may feel the effect. How you mark completion will depend on your personal style and circumstances.

CASE STUDY

At the height of the troubles in Northern Ireland, a troop of 45 men from the British Army went to West Belfast on an emergency tour. For four and a half months they lived in cramped conditions and did a job that was both tiring and potentially dangerous. They were involved in a number of incidents from riots to shootings. However, no-one was killed and there were no injuries beyond a few minor scrapes and bruises. By the end everyone was looking forward to getting home to their loved ones.

The week before they were due to leave, the troop sergeant suggested that on return to barracks the troop should stay together for a barbecue before dispersing. This would mean keeping the men in barracks for one extra night. Initially people were not keen on the idea, but in the end it went ahead and was much enjoyed (though scarcely remembered!) by all.

In the months that followed, the morale of the people who had been in that troop was uniformly high, while that of their colleagues was more variable. People who observed this attributed it to the fact that those without some event to mark the successful passing of a shared experience were still working out in their own minds whether it had been successful and worthwhile.

Ideas for celebrating success

How you decide to celebrate will depend on the size of your project team, the budget available and the nature of the project. The following list contains a number of creative ideas picked up from project managers. Whatever form of celebration you choose, bear in mind that, in all cases, it is the personal touch that people seem most to appreciate.

- Include a small celebration fund in the project budget, which can increase or decrease according to whether the project is ahead of or beyond its budget and schedule. Appoint a project "entertainment officer" to be responsible for deciding how the team will spend it at the end of the project.
- Give people an inscribed desk ornament to thank them for taking part. This does not have to be expensive or even tasteful.
- Have a team photograph taken and distributed at the end of the project.
- Frame an appropriate piece of the project plan for each team member and add a handwritten comment.
- Have a group caricature drawn, recalling your defining memories of each person, and give a copy to every team member.
- Hand write a personal thank-you letter to each team member. (People will swap notes, so make the effort to personalize each one.)
- Have a bottle of champagne sent to each team member's home with a suitable message or label.

6

Set up learning systems
Praise good work
Learn from mistakes
Publicize findings

What happened and why?
What can I learn from this?
What recommendations can I make?

Project review

Every project, regardless of whether it has been successful or not, should be viewed as an opportunity to learn. The review phase exists to help this happen. This chapter explains why it is worth taking the time to carry out a review, and offers some practical tips for gaining maximum return on the investment of time and energy that this involves.

When does review take place?

The review phase follows handover and is the last in the overall sequence of project phases. However, you may find it necessary to conduct periodic learning reviews at the end of key stages of your projects so that recommendations can be implemented without delay.

Carrying out a review

Irrespective of whether you are conducting an intermediate or final review, the more rigorous an approach you take, the more you, your team and your organization will benefit.

■ Consider the facts in detail. You need to ask yourself exactly what happened. Where this is not clear, obtain and carefully examine all the available evidence. When you have done this, take the time to make a balanced judgement.

■ Be curious. Ask yourself why these things happened. The answer will help you to decide whether the event was a "one-off" or can help you to deduce something that can be applied in future.

■ Follow through. Ask questions such as "Who will do what and by when to ensure that learning takes place?", and "Do we need to create a new capability to allow us to change the way we do something, or can we use the resources that we already have differently?"

The benefits of review

Carried out properly, a project review offers several benefits for the project manager, team members and the organization. Specifically it allows you to do all of the following.

1 Identify what went well and why

A review is not just about identifying and investigating errors. If a particular approach has worked well or a supplier or sub-contractor has performed outstandingly, this should be noted for the future.

2 Prevent errors being repeated

In any project, some things will go wrong and often these are unforeseeable the first time they occur. By taking time during the review phase to understand what has happened and why, you gain insights that would otherwise be missed. Next time round, the errors will be both foreseeable and avoidable.

3 Motivate project team members

People like to know how they've done, especially when they've put a lot of effort into a project. The review phase should include a summary of each person's performance. As long as you gather and disseminate information in the right way, you will find that people, particularly contractors, see project reviews as an excellent way of building their CV or portfolio of testimonials. Equally, people will be more likely to make an effort if they know that failure will be investigated and recorded.

To get maximum benefit from this aspect of the review, you should make sure that team members know in advance that their performance will be assessed at the end of the project. They should be clear about the criteria that will be applied and the form that feedback will take, and who else will receive this information.

"Don't blame, correct"

4 Stimulate ideas for further projects

The review phase should assess both the process and outcome of the project. During project work, team members may have become aware of issues that the project does not fully address, or areas where similar work needs to be done. The review therefore often acts as the catalyst for follow up projects.

Creating a culture of learning

Whatever the culture of your organization, as a project manager you are responsible for encouraging and modelling behaviour that supports learning within your project. You can do this in several ways.

1 Seek the value in people's observations and suggestions

Always be prepared to consider someone's ideas. If an idea coming from a member of your team is not immediately workable, use questions to help the person refine it. If this is not possible (perhaps it really is a dreadful idea!) tell them why this is the case. If ultimately you have to reject someone's idea, make it clear that you are not rejecting the process that led to them suggesting it in the first place. This leaves them free to make any new suggestions they may have.

2 Give people room to make mistakes

Your team can't learn if they are not allowed to try anything new. Be prepared to take calculated risks when giving people responsibilities within the project, and encourage them to do the same. Where things don't work out, help them to explore how they can avoid a repetition and seek an early opportunity to put this learning into practice.

3 Admit your own mistakes

Some project managers feel they should never make mistakes, so they hide them when they do occur. If you do this, you can expect the rest of your team to do the same. Learning cannot take place in these circumstances. Indeed there is a real danger that you will learn false lessons if people lie to cover up their mistakes. Let people see that you occasionally get things wrong, and they won't be afraid to admit that they do too.

4 Show excitement when you learn something new

Like the last point, this is a matter of setting an example to your team. If you pretend to know everything, your team members will think they have to, too, and will be reluctant to learn from one another as a result.

5 Allow others to build on your ideas

The most powerful level of organizational learning occurs when people are open to good ideas regardless of their source. Your ideas may be good, but they can often be improved by combining them with those of others. Lead by example: welcome ideas that build on your own. You will find others are far readier to be influenced by those around them.

Learning systems

A project review will have limited value unless you have a means of storing and disseminating the information it produces. If your organization does not yet have a system for doing this, you may wish to take a lead in setting one up.

What is a learning system?

A learning system needs to perform three functions.

- Gather the right information.
- Store it in an accessible format.
- Disseminate it to the appropriate people.

Gathering information

Learning may take place at any stage in a project, and the project manager should find some means of recording this. Some like to include "learning points" as an item on any project meeting agenda, so that team members can explain what they have learned and how others can apply it in future.

In addition, the final review of any project involving a team of people generally takes the form of a meeting or series of meetings, the minutes of which will form the core of a project review document.

Storing information

Review meetings usually generate three types of information.

- **Archive information**
  Information that may be needed to reconstruct past events – perhaps in the event of a legal dispute – but has little relevance for the future.

- **Reference information**
  Any information that may be of relevance to future projects. It should be stored in an easily accessible format and location.

- **Actions**
  Action points identified by the project reviews, such as changes that need to occur. These should always be allocated to specific people and have deadlines.

Disseminating information

An effective learning system must make people aware of new knowledge that is available. The project manager is responsible for publicizing the review findings, and may have to remind people of new information on several occasions before the message sinks in.

Most organizations are aware of only a fraction of the knowledge they have

Case study: learning systems

A large conference had run annually for five years by the time that Enda joined the team responsible for setting up and running the venue. Although he had considerable experience of running other events of this type, this was a voluntary organization, he was not the project manager, and he wanted to avoid upsetting the established leaders, so he simply got on with whatever he was asked to do, offering advice only when asked.

Gathering information

While keeping a low profile, Enda took note of every activity carried out by the team – when it was done, who did it and what materials were involved – in a small notebook that he kept constantly in his top pocket.

At the end of the conference there was the usual debriefing session for the project team. Referring to the records he had made, Enda offered a number of suggestions for improvements to the set-up process, most of which were readily adopted.

Applying learning

The following year, Enda was appointed site manager for the conference. Circumstances meant that he and his team had one less day in which to complete their work. Despite this and the late delivery of the sound and lighting equipment, by referring to the notes made the previous year, he and his team were able to complete the set-up process on time and at less cost.

The fruits of a good example

The clear value that Enda had derived from noting the activity sequence was not lost on the rest of the team. Most adopted a similar approach to their areas of responsibility and were able to identify numerous ways of improving use of resources that would not have been apparent to any single individual.

Reviewing individual performance

Project reviews often offer an excellent opportunity to focus on people's individual performance. The sponsor should offer feedback to the project manager, who should do the same for members of the project team. The assessment should take the form of a discussion, but you may also want to provide a written record.

Handling individual assessments

As with sub-contractors, individual team members may welcome a formal performance review at the end of the project as an opportunity to build their CV. Give them a clear assessment of how you saw their contribution, how well it was carried out, and whether they have developed new skills.

Of course, you may also have to give negative feedback, and this should be handled sensitively. The guidelines given here should help.

GIVING PERSONAL FEEDBACK

■ **SET LEARNING AND PERFORMANCE GOALS AT THE OUTSET**
Meaningful review must be prefaced by meaningful goal-setting.

■ **AGREE THE FORMAT, DISTRIBUTION AND TIMING OF ANY FEEDBACK**
If you plan to give written feedback, make it clear in advance that this will be the case.

■ **GIVE NEGATIVE FEEDBACK IN PERSON**
Never pass on negative feedback to a third party – for instance a person's manager – without telling the person involved first.

■ **MAKE FEEDBACK BALANCED, SPECIFIC AND ACTIONABLE**
Wherever possible, make it a dialogue. Often you will find the individual's insight into events goes beyond your own.

■ **REWARD SUCCESS IN AN APPROPRIATE WAY**
In some cases, positive feedback is reward enough in itself, but occasionally it will be necessary to back these up with more concrete measures such as promotion or a cash bonus.

Project review action points

Hold the final review meeting as soon as handover is complete

The usual response I get to this advice is that it is unrealistic or even impossible. However, the longer you leave a review, the more you are likely to have forgotten relevant facts and information by the time you get to it. Plan the review when you are planning the handover, and you should find it easier to get time in people's diaries.

Remember, holding an immediate review does not mean you cannot hold a second one later to confirm or change your recommendations once the dust has settled. Far from duplicating effort, you will find that you actually save time because memories are clearer and conclusions are reached more quickly.

Take time to plan the agenda

Be clear about which aspects of the projects you need to review. For a relatively small project, the agenda might be as simple as:
- What went well?
- What went badly?
- What would we do differently?
- Action points

For more complex projects, however, you will have many issues to address.

The checklist on page 92 outlines many of the questions you may need to ask.

Involve all stakeholders

Review should take account of the views of everyone involved. Naturally you need to balance this against practical restrictions on time and availability. Remember to include the views of the client/end user. In commercial projects you may need to think about how you will get these. It is often easier for the project sponsor to invite feedback on the day-to-day running of the project. If more impartial feedback is needed, you may choose to use a third party to conduct formal market research.

Be objective but sensitive

A "warts and all" appraisal of what happened can excite some fierce emotions if insensitively handled. Project reviews should never become witch-hunts. In order to engender an open dialogue, make it clear that negative feedback will not be broadcast. It is often a good idea to agree the wording and distribution of any learning points drawn from mistakes with those who made them.

Record your findings and recommendations succinctly

Write your review document with your reader in mind and make recommendations as brief as possible.

If you have to write a lot because the project was large and complex, structure the document in a way that enables people to gain an overview quickly and then select only the detail that is relevant to them.

You may decide to have more than one review document, so that people are not overwhelmed with a lot of information that is not relevant to them. A typical arrangement is to have a main document and a number of annexe documents.

The main document will include a number of key recommendations for the conduct of future projects. Distribute it widely to the team and other key stakeholders.

The annexe documents can either cover each recommendation in detail or provide more detailed feedback to specific individuals or departments. If you choose the latter format, it is often appropriate to distribute annexes to addressees only.

Discuss your recommendations with the project sponsor

The sponsor may want to be fully involved in the review process, but even if they do not, at the very least you should try and discuss the findings with him/her before disseminating them to a wider audience.

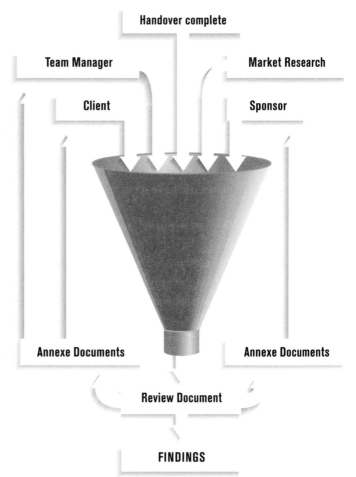

Project review checklist

1 Time

- How close to schedule did the project run?

- What variances occurred?

- Were there any areas in which we should have spent more time?

- What have we learned on scheduling?

2 Cost

- How close to cost was the project?

- What cost more/less than expected?

- Were there any areas in which we should have spent more money?

- Can we budget more accurately?

3 Quality

- Did the project as defined fulfil the client specification?

- How can specifications be more accurately written in future?

4 People

- Did people understand their roles?

- Was anyone over-employed or under-employed?

- How well did people work together?

- Did we have the right roles/skills within the project team?

- Was the process for monitoring performance successful?

- Were there any "people" issues that we can learn from?

5 Communications

- Were people sufficiently aware of progress?

- Were they quick to communicate any problems they had?

- Were any team members or stakeholders omitted from communications?

- How might communications be improved in any future project of this type?

6 Technology

■ What new technology was employed in this project?

■ How might technology have helped it run more smoothly?

7 Methodology

■ Did the project definition and planning phases work as expected?

■ What new tools and techniques have been developed?

■ What improvements might be useful?

■ How did the change monitoring and control process work?

■ Were the client and end user happy with the handover?

8 External suppliers

■ How did outside suppliers perform?

■ What can we learn from feedback on how we dealt with them?

■ What have we learned as a result of our dealings?

9 Overall

■ If I had the opportunity to do this project again what would I do differently?

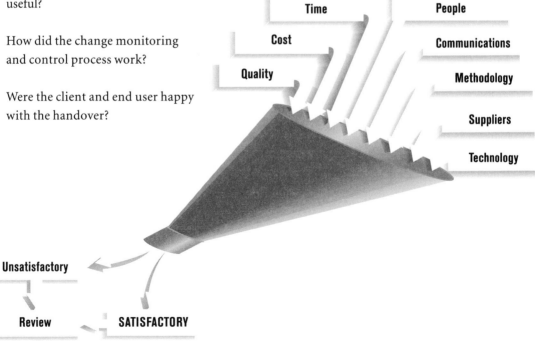

Index

Further reading

John Adair: *Effective Leadership* (Gower, 1983)

Roger Black: *Getting Things Done* (Penguin, 1991)

G. A. Cole: *Management Theory and Practice* (DP Publications, 1993)

Stephen Covey: *The Seven Habits of Highly Effective People* (Simon & Schuster, 1992)

Daniel Goleman: *Emotional Intelligence* (Bloomsbury, 1996)

Mack Hanan: *Consultative Selling* (Amacom, 1995)

David Hussey: *Strategy and Planning* (Wiley, 1999)

John Kao: *Jamming* (Harpercollins Business, 1996)

W. Chan Kim and René Mauborgne: "Fair Process" in *Harvard Business Review*, July/August 1997

Lorniman, Young and Kalinauckas: *Upside Down Management* (McGraw Hill, 1995)

Tom Peters: *The Tom Peters Seminar* (Random House, 1994)

Geoff Reiss: *Project Management Demystified* (E. & F. N. Spon, 1992)

J. Geoffrey Robinson: *Creative Thinking and Brainstorming* (Gower, 1989)

P. Senge: *The Fifth Discipline* (Century, 1990)